The Principles of the Bible

Johann Baptist Krebs

The Principles of the Bible

Johann Baptist Krebs

translated by Kerry A Nitz

K A Nitz
WHANGANUI, NEW ZEALAND

Die Grundzüge der Bibel
published in German 1838
under the pseudonym J. B. Kerning

This translation into New Zealand English
Copyright © K A Nitz 2024
All rights reserved

ISBN: 978-0-473-71484-0

Table of Contents

Translator's Note

For the English translation of Bible texts I have made use of the King James Version. Where I thought it would be helpful I have also inserted missing Biblical citations in the footnotes.

The occasionally somewhat idiosyncratic approach of the author to presenting dialogue has also been retained in part.

***

Preface

Called upon to publish his views over the principles of the Bible, the author of these pages decided to hand them over to the public, not in order to attack some system, or to speak out hostilely against a Bible interpretation, but rather with the intention of edifying, and of leading the person as much as possible from rough temporality into that paradisical region in which the tribal elders of all nations felt the peace of heaven and recognised in the innocence of an unspoilt disposition the conditions for immortality as certainly as we ourselves are conscious of the rising of the sun.

With this plan it could not be escaped that comparisons with other writings would have to be raised which bear the appearance of a criticism in themselves; only this happened not only to illuminate such, but rather to give the task before us greater comprehensibility. According to the view which is put forward in these pages, the Bible tolerates no limitation or paraphrasing of its content; just as the thing is given, so must it prove to be, or the Bible has stopped being a holy book.

After these short intimations, despite the caveat, nevertheless everybody will think it is looking for a small battle. It is true, without certain writings these pages would not have been written. Irrespective of them, the author feels free of any hostile thoughts, he hopes to the contrary to draw the dissenter to his interest and to give him an opportunity to illuminate yet more brightly with the sharpness of the mind the path described here and to also make the proper sacrifice to the truth in this way.

There is only *one* truth. All to whom life is more than a vegetative process seek it. It is therefore not the thing which is being disputed here, but rather the means of achieving it. Others specify such means on the strength of their own powers of thought; in these pages nature and the Bible were used in order by means of their authority to lay a thread for thorough investigation.

Humans belong to two worlds, the temporal and the eternal. Anyone who lives only in the first will never obtain exact knowledge of the second. But anyone who wanted in the here and now to go over to the second completely would block off many sources of knowledge. Humans belong to both, they have obligations to both; only when they fulfil these will the true light, the light of eternity rise for them, and show them the path of immortality which they are ordained to walk on by the creator.

In the lively conviction of this the author considered himself obligated to have his light shine, even if still so small, not just to guide himself, but rather to put in the hands of more seasoned thinkers the means to smooth the indicated path and to make it passable for many wanderers.

And consequently, little booklet, seek your path! Harm nobody, instead refresh! And should someone who is of an entirely different mind set eyes on you, then penetrate into his heart so that, grasped by your suggestions, he happily renders homage to the higher nature of the human and recognises in his nobler self his home again. Wander your path and pour peace into many a breast so that one learns to feel that the human does not find heaven outside himself, but rather only within himself.

***

Part 1: The Lord's Prayer

1. The Business Profession

The son of a rich merchant in Hamburg showed from youth onwards a great disposition for scientific learning. His father, who would rather have seen him trained in the safe money business, finally gave way to his son's inclination, since he had two sons, and let him attend university after completing his preparatory studies.

The expectations for which his aptitudes had raised hope were completely justified, for when he passed his legal exams after four years he received the general testimony that it had not been for many years that any student of Themis* had left the university with such thorough knowledge.

Now to already enter into the service of his father's city or an allied state seemed to him and his family too early; it was therefore decided to send him on a tour in order to collect experience of foreign lands and the knowledge of human character which would have to be profitable for him in any career which he were to enter in future. Since one was not short of money for travel, the itinerary merely had to be drawn up, the necessary letters of introduction obtained, and then put into effect.

First he visited the main cities of Germany and spent as long in each of them as the locality offered nourishment to his thirst for knowledge. After he had seen and heard everything in this way, at the same time having made the acquaintance of

---

* [Tr.: Greek goddess of order and justice.]

the distinguished men, he went to Italy to investigate there the history of his subject as it were in the cradle.

Italy indeed did not offer him in respect to his science what he had expected, only the stay in Rome and other cities of this European paradise with its monuments and art treasures gave his life views a new, elevated direction so that he could only part with effort from such palaces, churches, and magical regions after a stay of two years. But finally, since the letters of his family admonished him constantly to not forget the travel itinerary, he embarked at Palermo, sailed through the Strait of Gibraltar and stepped after a short happy journey onto England's soil.

As much to begin with as the coldness of these island inhabitants deterred him, he could not deny his homage to their solidity. He saw here in practice much which in other lands was still written and spoken about as hypotheses, and declared the English to be the deepest thinkers, and in respect to constitutional law and natural law to be the number one model for governments and universities.

From England he travelled by ship over to France. Here he stepped, according to his own judgement, into a new world. He found neither the ardour of the Italians, nor the solidity of the English, but rather a race of men who spoke in the highest animation about everything, undertook everything, but because of all their views on life they arrived at no results nor peace. His money and credit obtained him entrance everywhere, and he saw himself, before two months had passed, in a whirl of acquaintances and pleasures of life which left him no time to spend on positive scientific investigations and observations.

For almost an entire year he swam in this current, and the waves would probably have swallowed him up if the repeated and earnest commands of his father to return home had not arrived. You are in the land of the sirens, he said in his last letter; block your ears and come to us before they entice you overboard and poison your heart. He respected the words of his father and hurried back into the arms of his family.

He felt wondrously moved when he entered the house of his father again after an absence of four years. With emotion he greeted his father who had supported him so richly and granted him what so many upright youths had to do without, to get to know men amongst men and the world through his own experience.

Now it was time to give his life course a specific direction and not to lock away the fruits of his knowledge, but rather to use it to the best for others. But in what way? On what paths? Over that much was thought, much spoken, but for a long time no decision taken.

Bonhardt frequently discussed with his father the choice of his future sphere of business. "What paths lie before me?", he once uttered during such a conversation. "How can I most confidently satisfy the urge to be of use to the city of my birth or, if it is possible, to humanity? Should I apply to the Senate for a position? That leads to a distinguished path which must be walked in a mechanical direction without looking forward or to the sides. Should I offer myself to the citizenry to exercise my overview and acumen in entangled legal cases? I cannot see this as my life's goal either. I have long since formed my own philosophy of professional activity in general and in specifics. According to this three paths lie open before us, on the one of which we are forced to wander. On the first the law of necessity reigns where that which we do must happen if a gap should not arise. The next shows us usefulness as the palm tree of life. Here you work in constantly fresh liveliness because in all circumstances that which brings profit is welcome and at the same time obligatory. On the third path are found the roses of existence which lend to everything the man undertakes the stimulus of grace and makes you forget the thorns which often scratch our skin. Now I ask, on which path should I begin my business voyage and where do I find the means of being permitted to wander it according to my mind?"

His father did not give any decisive judgement during such conversations and left it to his son to freely make his choice. The latter contemplated when he was alone once more the principles of his professional philosophy and said to himself, "In the realm of beauty I will indeed find roses, but no fruit; fruit grow in the areas of usefulness and necessity. Arts are lovely stars, but they have already enticed many of their disciples and adherents into the abyss, meanwhile others, without knowing them, achieve their life's goal; they dispense accordingly with every necessary demand and are only for the weak who must be drawn to good by means of stimulus. Away from this realm! May its flowers bloom, I will waste neither time nor effort planting them.

Usefulness, what are you? A tree from which poor and rich, guilty and innocent, happy and sad pluck. To you is dedicated pure humanness, but not the goal of humanity, because on your path the avaricious walk with the spendthrift and the rogue with the honest citizen.

In necessity all requirements of our activity dissolve themselves. What is not necessary can also remain undone without a creature, or any part of creation being vitally endangered. Those who feel strong in themselves must dedicate themselves to the necessity of dispensing with passing means of stimulus."

More weeks went past amidst such contemplations, when he learnt that a case between a rich man and a poor man had turned out in favour of the former because through money he could set in motion more capable lawyers. Here Bonhardt cried out instinctively, "The poor must be supported against the rich, that is a necessity, and hence I must not remain idle any longer."

The next day he had himself registered as a practitioner of law with the declaration of conducting all cases of the poorer class without charge and if need be at his own cost.

In a short time he had so much to do that he obtained no time to think to himself. "I am not living for myself in the present circumstances anymore, but rather for others," he said one day after arduous work, "and am a cosmopolitan in the strictest sense. But does the man belong", he continued, "then unconditionally to others and does he not also have rights for himself and obligations to himself?"

With this question he still owed himself, as often as he repeated it too, an answer.

It is a strange thing about man, he often thought; quickly resolved to do everything good for others, for himself he finds neither impetus nor time. Should there not yet be a goal, a duty for the man which is mirrored not in the reflection of the works for others, but rather within himself? Is the man made for himself or for others? Has the other more worth when I help him, and does my worth rise to the degree of the help provided? Giving help and receiving help, is this the natural and necessary division of the human race? You may consider this question however you like, on the one side lies something humiliating and on the other something overbearing, as if you wanted to say to the one, "you must help", and to the other, "you must be helped".

It is not a question that to stand by those in need of help seems to be the law of nature, but making such the goal of your existence has the form of an arrogance which enjoys itself only in the imposition of its will on others. The man is certainly, like every other creature, first and foremost present for himself and only when he has obtained in this respect some maturity and independence should he then be permitted to think of having an effect for others and on others.

Is there a human race which, born as child, would only be capable of living through others? Has not nature opened to everyone its springs? Would it, this infinitely kind mother, have damned the greater half of its children to only exist through the help of others in uninterrupted dependency? That would be unjustly hard and cruel. Nature is not unjust, but men are from inertia, pride, and weakness. Hence let every man act and work, and only if he is completely incapable of helping himself, lend him your arm and guide him like you guide a blind man, even sometimes a drunk.

He considered his sacrifice for others in the same way now, and came to the conclusion that he had previously missed the vocation of his life while he had given support for six years to the wilfully impoverished, the litigation-addicted, and occasionally fraudsters. Are these, he asked himself, the fruits of my virtue which I had imagined conditioned by a sort of necessity? If standing by others, if science and arts deliver no certain results, where can I then seek further?

One field is left to which I have never had the courage to turn my gaze, theology; this I have constantly considered to be the severest of all that is given, which does not allow a line of deviation without destroying the whole. Theology! Divine doctrine! Knowledge of God! It makes me faint when I want to gather these ideas into concepts. Knowledge of God! Divine doctrine! — The clergyman is called to inquire into the nature of God and to disperse it amongst his listeners. Sublime profession when it is fulfilled, or is to be fulfilled!

If it is to be fulfilled! Herein lies the evil that you have become doubtful over the possibility of fulfillment. All examples which come from this school believe with what has been learnt by heart to possess the spirit, torment the people with given phrases and sayings and shout damnation over those who do not believe them blindly.

Where is the goal of life? In this goal all threads should unite which are laid through life for us.

We wander through life, must wander without rest and standstill. Are threads laid for us which will show us the way? Or are we exposed to chance? If it is the first then necessity demands we get to know it; if it is the second then all ideas of perfection disappear, and the man with his brilliant gifts for arts, science, and skilfulness is a bubble filled with shimmering mist which parts when the bubble bursts.

Goal of man, how does one recognise you? Self-knowledge, said the ancients, leads to wisdom and this to life.

Here is the point which would be discussed if it is to be discussed. Wisdom, what is it? In no school do you hear it being defined. If it belongs under the sciences, it must be taught and dealt with somewhere though; but the most erudite professors go past it so timidly when it accidentally comes up, as if they were frightened to come into contact with it.

Wisdom, you exist, otherwise you would not be named. In the most elevated books you are spoken of, you are referenced. Indeed a positive doctrine to win you is found nowhere, but intimations are present to create a doctrine perhaps. Probably, the attempt may decide; you can only get to know a foreign region if you travel around it.

From now on he gave up all business for the bourgeois life, ordered books which seemed to be suited to his plan, and read so much that he believed himself justified in the belief of having found the way; but when he compared the gathered fruits with the laws of reason, his courage fell again and he was close to considering the entire thing to be an ideal fiction and man to be incapable of such a high good.

Knowledge of God, he said as he took up the subject again, is certainly the peak of wisdom, is its essence, its goal. But how do you obtain it? What gives us the proof of whether we stand on the point which allows no deception anymore? Self-deception is the evil which seduced so many, misled to fanaticism and intolerance, outraged nations and brought horror and destruction amongst humanity. Only one sure test proves to the reckoner whether he calculated correctly: what is the test of wisdom?

He cried out, I must obtain light for myself! I must know whether there is something to investigate here, and should I set the efforts of my life to it. Theology gives knowledge of God, knowledge of God is wisdom, who can help but those whose profession it is to get to the bottom of the matter? And who else would this be than the theologians whose contact I have previously avoided from a sort of prejudice because I suspected in their studies only the given and no philosophical necessity? I must make good my mistake and catch up on what I have neglected. Even if they are not in the light of wisdom, they possess a system though, the skeleton of it, and who knows whether it is not possible to bring life into it. Hence away with everything which I have learnt and done up to now, the highest, the necessary thing which raises man to man and leads him to the end goal of his existence must be granted to me, only then can life be of value to me and award me what I seek, certainty over the relationship in which I stand to God and nature.

***

2. The Profession of Man

Bonhardt's father had meanwhile died and had left behind for his three sons a means of two million marks. The two others continued the father's business, but the legal scholar placed his inheritance in secure interest, firmly resolved to live independently from now on and to dedicate himself to the study of the purest philosophy, of wisdom.

To achieve his goal more securely, he had himself introduced into the company of such clergymen who stood in the repute of a higher knowledge of God. They took him up with love, extolled to him the blessedness of a life dedicated to God and revealed to him, when he spoke about wisdom, frankly that it was not a branch of human cleverness and science, but rather a gift of God, provided through his holy spirit to all those who ardently sigh for it and have steady faith.

Bonhardt listened to such utterances with self-sacrificing doggedness in the hope of finally finding a connecting thread for his actions. He sighed with ardour after that spirit which would be capable of imparting to him wisdom. But when his efforts remained without success, he said glumly, "What am I obtaining for my sacrifice? Nothing but the conviction that I will not find what I am seeking here either. The clergy lead me to a certain point and say, 'Here is the dividing wall, our eyes cannot penetrate any further; what is behind it is not to be described, but rather only recognised through faith.'

Where is truth here? Where a light to disperse the night which envelops me? I should believe? And what? And whom?

But what if I cannot believe? If that which I should believe contradicts my way of thinking? Thus it stands written, say the priests. What! And because it stands written, I should have to believe! And this faith, what does it offer me in my thirst for truth? The more I endeavour to believe, the narrower becomes the field of my prospects, so that I now hardly make out anymore the dividing wall which I previously glimpsed and see myself robbed of everything which could impart a higher worth to life."

One day he travelled into the countryside. The solitude of the tavern where he was spending his midday seemed suited to increasing the feeling of his hopelessness. He had barely the courage still to think about the object of his wishes, far less to speak about them. When they were already wanting to serve his midday meal, a traveller stopped before the tavern. A country clergyman of mature years, but friendly appearance climbed down from a one-horse carriage and after a few minutes stepped into the tavern. Since the table of honour was set for Bonhardt, the landlady asked whether he would not allow the arrival to also be permitted to be waited on there. He understandably gave his assent and thus he and the clergyman took their midday meal together.

To begin with they said nothing at all, later speaking of trivial things, but when the tavern staff and the few guests who were present had left, Bonhardt could not withstand the desire to speak about theology with his table companion. The latter indeed gave seemingly indifferent answers, only in these Bonhardt, who had already obtained a dexterity in respect to theological utterances, noticed a difference between what he was hearing now and what he had heard before. "We must become more closely acquainted", he said full of happy confidence. "I am striving for truth, and to achieve my goal more securely I turned to the theologians, but I arrived at an artificial fountain which flows only so long as you pour water from above into the pipes. If you are the man who can be of help in my investigations, then I ask you to instruct me, and you will be convinced that thankfulness still resides amongst humanity."

The clergyman look at him for a few moments with searching eyes, and said, "You seem to be rich?"

22

Bonhardt: "Yes."

Clergyman: "And yet you strive for truth?"

Bonhardt: "Yes."

Clergyman: "What moves you to do so?"

Bonhardt: "The wish to be acquainted with the destiny of humanity."

Clergyman: "You do not know it?"

Bonhardt: "No."

Clergyman: "Has school, experience, or the clergy not instructed you about it?"

Bonhardt: "School kept silent about it. Experience teaches us world events, shows us struggles about seemingly good things. The clergy led to the dividing wall behind which the eye of the mortal can and must not look."

Clergyman: "Do you believe that?"

Bonhardt: "No."

Clergyman: "What do you believe then?"

Bonhardt: "Sometimes a lot, sometimes nothing at all."

Clergyman: "What do you mean by that?"

Bonhardt: "When I am seized by the wonders of creation, I believe a lot; but when I consider humans, as they come and go, chivy and chase, are afraid and torment themselves, and nowhere find a goal, how all strive only to spice the present in order to make it properly enjoyable, then the feeling of my faith loses itself so much that I feel dizzy to live and I see in myself the reflection of a light which illuminates me sparingly today, but tomorrow is extinguished."

Clergyman: "You are tied to business?"

Bonhardt: "I have freed myself from it."

Clergyman: "So without profession?"

Bonhardt: "Not entirely; I am taking myself to school."

Clergyman: "And learning?"

Bonhardt: "I have no plan yet."

Clergyman: "Why do you not draft one up?"

Bonhardt: "How can I when I do not know yet what I should learn?"

Clergyman: "There are so many objects; choose."

Bonhardt: "The absolutely right one cannot be an object, it must be a thing which encloses everything within itself."

Clergyman: "Everything that exists is an object."

Bonhardt: "And yet there must be something which is so high above everything that you cannot call it an object anymore."

Clergyman: "I would know of nothing of that sort."

Bonhardt: "God is not an object anymore because everything is contained in him."

Clergyman: "You can make God into the object of his considerations?"

Bonhardt: "Quite right. But then the object is a two-sided concept because it describes something which is not comprehended and yet must be spoken of."

Clergyman: "In such a way we must keep to that which can be discussed, and this remains an object."

Bonhardt: "It is then not a single object, but rather it develops objects which in their totality could again become one object if we had a band to connect them."

Clergyman: "And such a band, you think, is not to be found?"

Bonhardt: "I do not know."

Clergyman: "How do you get to know a thing?"

Bonhardt: "Through the feel of its effect on us."

Clergyman: "And do you consider it impossible to feel God?"

Bonhardt: "What we feel is physical, but God is spirit."

Clergyman: "He could not, you think, be felt as spirit?"

Bonhardt: "Probably not."

Clergyman: "The spiritual is more certain to be felt than the physical."

Bonhardt: "That I cannot see."

Clergyman: "Only the spiritual feels, thus it must also be felt."

Bonhardt: "This conclusion is an hypothesis."

Clergyman: "But it isn't, it encloses the purest necessity within itself."

Bonhardt: "May I ask for an explanation."

Clergyman: "There are things of which we say that they are without smell, taste, form, or colour; that which differentiates itself through smell, taste, form, or colour has separated itself from chaos and stands there in a particular being and spirit."

Bonhardt: "But sound, colour, form, taste, and smell are bound to physical things, thus themselves physical."

Clergyman: "The feelings of love arises through agreeing, ingratiating demeanours and gestures, are they therefore physical?"

Bonhardt: "If they must be stirred by physical impressions, quite certainly."

Clergyman: "If we consider the beginnings of the purest thought and judgement, we find their roots always in the physical world. Indeed even if we wanted to think — nothing — we would have to allocate a place for the nothing in which it would be surrounded by things which are physical. In such a way we could not think the nothing to be unphysical."

Bonhardt: "So it seems."

Clergyman: "You would like spiritual effects without contact with anything physical?""

Bonhardt: "Yes."

Clergyman: "And with this the dividing wall is described before which you stand and which, according to your way of investigating, can never be broken through. This is the sore point of all limited thinkers who fear the proximity of God and his spirit, disembody him and thereby distance him from the creation and the created. God is everywhere, in us, around us, and we in him. As the lungs breathe in the air and nourish themselves with it, so do all inner organs, even the marrow in the bones, breathe in higher and purer air, and nourish themselves with it for the spiritual life. Where is their a division here? Where a standstill? Everything works and strives in perfect hierarchy and connection to a goal, to one aim."

Bonhardt: "But in this way all spiritual freedom ceases, and positive spiritual power separate from the physical world is an empty idea."

Clergyman: "So it is. The great mass seeks spiritual power in the absolute nothingness. The free investigator sees form everywhere and spirit everywhere."

Bonhardt: "Is this doctrine able to be put to use?"

Clergyman: "Only in this way is practical use possible."

Bonhardt: "And God's omnipotence should be recognised in such division, such isolating?"

Clergyman: "Can you imagine the order and the course of the stars in the sky?"

Bonhardt: "With means of assistance, yes, but without such, no."

Clergyman: "And you think to be able to imagine God's omnipotence and greatness when you are incapable of making clear the seasons of the earth and the course of the moon without pen and paper. A mediation between God and us is necessary if we want to arrive at knowledge of him, and this mediation is us, is the human, his form, his language, and the thirst for divine revelation, be it through the word in us, or through the effect on the course of our life."

Bonhardt: "You surprise me and seem forcibly before my eyes to want to break through the dividing wall at which I stand. I have never considered the matter from this side. I am like the child who desires to be led up the mountain in order to play with the moon. Mediation is according to such a view grounded in nature and the human is the miniature model of the endlessness of God. I must confess, after what I have heard I have won hope and perceive the mistakes to which we draw ourselves laboriously when in working ourselves up we intensify more and more the idea of God and finally come to the point where we lose him entirely from our sight. I thank you for your discussion and beg you to instruct me further so that the little bit of light which you have kindled in me does not go out again."

The clergyman assured him of the greatest willingness to unveil to him everything for which he made himself fit, and asked him to meet with him again in fourteen days in that tavern, because he himself would be there again about that time on business.

They conversed for a while yet over the above mentioned views and confusions which had to necessarily arise when you undertook to investigate God in his generality or in a mediated state entirely outside us. These mistakes, the clergyman said, are the cause of why we do not possess any pure divine doctrine anymore and defend the little bit that is given with stubbornness and fanaticism. The human is directed to himself, even according to the words of Christ. He is the measure of his knowledge and the drawing board on which he finds all the relationships between God and nature drawn up.

Amidst such conversation Bonhardt was initiated ever more deeply into the doctrine that was foreign to him, so that when they parted he said with full confidence, "You have opened the dividing wall which separated me from the holy of holies of humanity, this gives me the grounded hope that you will lead me on the path begun which will guide me to the land of purest knowledge."

***

3. The Art of Praying

Bonhardt sought in every possible way to fortify in himself the idea of attaining knowledge of God through himself. To this end he kept from the moment in which this became clear to himself his own journal devoted to it, in order to write down what he had heard and what he had thought himself. One morning, as his soul was full of feeling of the omnipresence of God, he wrote the following.

God is the universe. He is it. You cannot say God is in the universe or the universe in God, otherwise we separate ourselves and the creation from him and him from us. Does not every uninhibited eye see a division there which must lead by necessity to errors. God is the eternal unity and can never be two with respect to his nature.

Indeed, the human stands there as his own ego and decides and acts arbitrarily. From where does this freedom come? Perhaps from outside himself? If powers did not lie in nature in which such arbitrariness is contained, he could not have it either. The human remains therefore, even if not so free, yet constantly only the handmaid of the powers conferred on him.

The universe is God, the human is a part of the universe, consequently also a part of God. Can the part surely overlook the whole? To the extent it is a part, it can perceive some, but incomplete parts do not see much. What is the human? Does he belong to the complete or the incomplete parts? As we consider the matter, it follows that self-knowledge is the necessary condition for obtaining the truth.

The fourteen days were over. Bonhardt and the clergyman came together in the designated tavern. The former revealed the new views and doubts he had obtained, and asked the latter to give him an assured standpoint for judging his investigations. The clergyman said, "You must learn to pray."
Bonhardt: "Pray! What should I pray and how?"
Clergyman: "The Lord's Prayer*."
Bonhardt: "And this prayer?"
Clergyman: "Is guide and teacher, if you understand how to pray in it in the spirit."
Bonhardt: "I have often admired the extensiveness of its content, but not found in it such practical use."
Clergyman: "And nevertheless it can only be understood practically."
Bonhardt: "I am eager for the more detailed explanation."
Clergyman: "Then listen.
First petition: Our Father, which art in heaven.
We call God father because he created all things and called the human to life from chaos. In this respect he is the father of all that which is, from the purest cherub to the insect, from the starry sky with all its suns and worlds to the speck of dust which our eye barely sees. The creator certainly finds himself in this fatherhood towards humans, but the idea of it is so great that the one born of dust is not capable of grasping it in the myriad of parts. For this reason God must, if we shall truly nurse child-like feelings for him, be moved closer to us so that, like the child to the loving father, we grow close to him and can transfer to him the guidance of our fate full of cheer. It is easy to say father, but to feel child-like, to fear like a child, to hope and to love like a child is a state where the noblest characteristics of the human must be drawn to the light. It thus becomes necessary to first seek the fatherhood of God and to become worthy of it, before we are in a state to comprehend this prayer only to some extent. It is likewise when we say: which art in heaven. We see the blue mantle of

---

*   [Tr.: Matthew 6:9–13, Luke 11:2–4. The version from Matthew has been used throughout.]

the horizon; the uneducated says that is the heaven. Above this blue mantle are countless stars which lose themselves in the endlessness and leave us with just the inkling of ever new, invisible worlds. This immeasurability is certainly also the heaven, but not that which the child says to the father, which art in heaven. The boundless universe cannot be meant here; there must be a heaven which agrees with our limitedness, in which we seek the father as our benefactor and provider and can give ourselves over to his love in child-like trust.

Second petition: Hallowed be thy name.

What is God called? What is his name? In the knowledge of this lies the quintessence of life, the ordination of human nature, without which everybody should be afraid to write a book, accept a teaching position or a pulpit.

That it is not the word *God* that is understood by this is clear; for this is not a name, but rather an arbitrary conceptual designation to indicate what you are speaking of. Likewise it is not about the word *father* which designates a characteristic and also cannot be a name. The name of God is the root of the original language, is that word which is God and through which everything was made which is made.

Third petition: Thy kingdom come.

The kingdom of the father which art in heaven shall come to us, be granted to us. Here you again run into a knot which is only to be unravelled with the greatest effort. There is talk of a kingdom which is in heaven because the father also resides in heaven. The kingdom and heaven seem according to the placement of both petitions do be two different things, and yet they must not be separated if we do not want to make two different beings from the father. Both belong to the father, heaven and the kingdom. Both are only one thing, and yet they must be thought of as different things. Heaven is the great whole which extends through eternity; the kingdom, however, is in it, but just as immeasurable and unbounded. It is the inner light of heaven, the animating and spiritual power from which thoughts germinate and from which the human rises to God, the father. Both are infinite in space and time, and poured into one another in such a way that they, like blood and life, comprise only one thing and there where heaven is, the kingdom is too, and where kingdom is, heaven is too. Thy kingdom come means accordingly: give us the light which fills heaven and make it the residence for your glory.

Fourth Petition: Thy will be done in earth, as it is in heaven.

What is the will of the father? Where do we learn to recognise it? That a written book can express the will of the eternal and the laws of eternity points to a limitedness of the thinking which only our age is capable of passing over. In earlier times, even in the first blossoming of Christianity, it was law to still possess next to the written word the living word in order to comply with the will of God all the more certainly. Thy will be done in earth, as it is in heaven was thus a demand to those spiritual guides to get to know the will of God which is exercised in heaven and to then make use of it on earth. So it was formerly, now it is different. Today we scream about that time: darkness! Those times prophesied our time and they described it as a falling away from the spirit and the eternal truth."

Bonhardt had been listening with great attentiveness. Now he said, "If that is the meaning of the Lord's Prayer, then I deplore the entirety of Christianity who rattle it off without understanding and feeling. What you are saying to me is so new that I must think about whether I am understanding it correctly and whether the explanation stands in real or only apparent agreement with the thing. Allow me therefore, before you speak further, to repeat the entirety in order to secure myself through your reprimand from any self-deception."

The clergyman listened calmly, corrected what did not agree with what had been said, or was not clear enough, and promised him at their next meeting to give an explanation of the subsequent petitions in order thereby to put him in a position to see over the whole and to draw the results from it which anybody can achieve who makes the attempt with earnestness and practical exercise.

They parted with the agreement to see each other in the same tavern in fourteen days when the clergyman again had business to deal with in the area.

Bonhardt used this time to think over what he had heard and to order it in his own manner. We here take his own words from the above mentioned journal.

I have heard and read much, have practised analysing the most difficult tasks syllogistically, now a theme lies before me whose nature I do not sense and is so foreign to me, as if I had to unlock a magical lock whose opening no eye has seen. Where do I begin? And how do I begin? Under what forms can I bring ideas which, as it were coming from eternity, guide us there again? I should learn to pray! And what? The Lord's Prayer: Our Father, which art in heaven. God is my father, he is in heaven; and I! Where am I then? Is heaven around me and I already in it in the here and now? The Bible says: Heaven cometh not with observation: Neither shall they say, Lo here! or, lo there! for, behold, it is in the hearts of men.[*]

If heaven is in the heart, the father must be in it too. But what is he doing in the hearts of those born of dust? If we consider the natural circumstances of a father, he is a begetter, nourisher, and educator of the son. To think of God as begetter is certainly strange, for what could he beget in us? Perhaps a new, divine man who would be born in us to a higher life? Except a man be born again in the spirit, the Bible says further, he cannot see the kingdom of God.[†] But in what relation then does the natural, first-born man stand to the father and his divine son? The thoughts are flying in me. The answer lies on my lips, but I shy from putting it into words. And yet it must be said! I write for myself and the truth: — The relationship in which the natural man stands to the eternal father and to the divine son would be the relationship of a mother to father and son.

---

[*]   [Tr.: Luke 17:20–21 actually states "The kingdom of God cometh not with observation: Neither shall they say, Lo here! or, lo there! for, behold, the kingdom of God is within you". The German text deviates from Luther's Bible in a similar way.]

[†]   [Tr.: John 3:3. The "in the spirit" is in the Bible of Luther, but not in the King James Version.]

Holy thought of God! Sublime relationship if the man could enclose himself with such eternal bonds of love and fuse himself with the father and the divine son so intimately.

May I devote myself to these thoughts? Is a possibility present to ever make them clear, convincing? Here I feel the weakness of human nature which with all the consequences of the ideas cannot grasp the matter because it stands too far above the usual powers of thought. Where to begin now? What means to grasp in order to not get dizzy?

Here faith is necessary. With the fullest certainty faith must not be lacking, otherwise it turns into a blinding light which destroys the mind. In faith, which I have already denied so often, I must take refuge so that I do not become too weak for further investigation.

I must pass over to the second petition; in the first I am losing myself as if I were in a labyrinth where I guess at the exit, but do not see the way.

Hallowed be thy name.

Here the powers of thought and imagination fall silent. If this petition contains reality, then I do not know where to begin and where to end.

The son should know the name of the father though. Father is not a name, God just as little. A great lord can be father and king, yet he must still have a name.

History does not teach me anything, the Bible does not either. Where will I find light in this chaos.

Pythagoras speaks of a Pythia, of a Pytha. The Indians praise the name Ixora* as the root of all being. The Israelites also possess a name which they know, but never speak aloud. What are these names? What do they mean?

It cannot be about meaning here, but rather about being. "In the beginning was the Word, and the Word was with God, and the Word was God."† This sounds like an unsolvable puzzle. Further, "All things were

---

*   [Tr.: Ishvara or Shiva.]
†   [Tr.: John 1:1.]

made by the same; and without the same was not any thing made that was made."* I must ask here simply, through what is everything made? According to the placement of the words: through the word. God is the word, the word is God, thus the word is creator and tool of creation at the same time. "In him (in the word) was life; and the life was the light of men. And the light shineth in darkness."† There lies the hieroglyph in which life, power, and wisdom seem to be contained, but in the way that it is only then possible to explain the puzzle of the sphinx when the sacrifices of all who have fallen were comprehended in its dark words.

If God is the word, then this word is also the name of God. What word is it though? Is it arbitrarily put together, or like the stepladder of the numbers and tones grounded in eternal laws? It must be the latter because God, who is there what he is, allows no arbitrariness, knows no accident, but rather exists unwavering in his being.

Eternal name! I want to hallow you without knowing you; is this not enough for you? — Blind delusion! Vain form! How can I hallow without knowledge! — Through faith, the priest says. But I cannot believe without knowledge, because I am indeed myself in need of believing the knowledge of that which I recognise.

It sounds puzzling, and yet it is so — the faith must remain, even with the knowledge, because this exceeds the measure of common knowledge so much that faith must renew it for evermore. But where do I find the intimated knowledge? Who will give me the key to open the entrance. — Music in its uncountable works has only one chord; you could call this, if music were spheres, by the name of Apollo. The art of calculating has only ten digits, with these it divides, doubles, quadruples, and cubes myriads of units. If calculating were

---

*   [Tr.: John 1:3. The King James Version has "him" where Luther's Bible has the equivalent of "the same". Thus the King James Version is "All things were made by him and without him was not any thing made that was made", and here I have used a composite of the two translations.]

†   [Tr.: John 1:4–5.]

speaking, the name of the creator of the art of calculation would consist of the ten units. Where is the root of the word or of languages? We hear speaking indeed, we see the characters of languages, but we are through hearing and seeing still left to arbitrariness — where is the root of language which sends us from eternity germs and fruits which are so little to be altered as numbers and tones, and which is there what it is, like God who is the word?

I cannot inquire any further. I feel my power of thought flagging in these regions. I seem to myself to be like a child who has the desire and the courage to climb a high mountain, but already worn out at the twentieth part of the way cannot go any further. I do not find light anywhere and must wait for my guide. Need the human always have a guide then? Is his nature not built on its own foundation? Can it not mature through itself like everything else? What I have yet learnt and practised is, even if with effort, to be derived from a principle, a law, in short a root — shall then there be no beginning and no end here? — I cannot reach it myself. Human nature, despite its glorious talents, seems to be destined to have to languish in dependency and to beg from others.

"Thy kingdom come" is the third petition.

Where do I find the kingdom of that one who for me still has no name? I can repeat after the clergyman the petition word for word, but find no trace of any connection drawn from within myself. Heaven is the region, the kingdom, the community erected and ruled through the law. What is the law? Where is the community? To distinguish one kingdom from another we must have recognised the regent and his form of rule, otherwise we are in complete ignorance and cannot profess ourselves to be members of it without sacrilegious arrogance. I know neither regent nor kingdom, thus I must not dare more than to say: the kingdom in heaven shall also become my fatherland.

The fourth petition is "Thy will be done in earth, as it is in heaven."

Here I must fall silent. How can the will of a ruler be carried out, if we do not know his kingdom and its name. I must wait for instruction like the child who attends school for the second time, and barely knows yet that the schoolmaster has set him a task.

***

4. Continuation of the Prayer

Finally the yearned for day arrived on which he and the clergyman had agreed to see each other again. He had already been on the spot a long time before the latter arrived in a one horse carriage. When he saw the familiar vehicle in the distance, he went in front of the tavern, greeted it like a lover greeting the beloved, and helped take care of the necessities of the horse in order to be able to speak with him as soon as possible. They had barely stepped into the room when he handed over his journal to explain his incapability, as he expressed it, of arriving at a result in such pure, spiritual tasks. The clergyman read it with pleasure and said finally, "If logical conclusions were capable of leading to a goal, then you would have to succeed; but since such is not possible, since matters of feeling, especially living powers are not to be dissected, the finest syllogistic breaks down when it dares to enter this space. When you now listen to the fifth petition, it will give you clearer hints of the omnipresence of God and his influence on us.

Fifth petition: Give us this day our daily bread.

Here the prayer begins to become practical and to encroach on our life circumstances. We must learn to recognise the hand of God, to factually convince ourselves that he attends to us, provides for us, and offers us the primary needs of life. Give us this day our daily bread is the first petition of the child to the father, because without bread no life existence is possible. It is accordingly the beginning here of where the human asserts his being child of the fatherhood of God and asks him for that which every father is obliged to give the child."

"But who reminds", Bonhardt asked quickly, "the father if he considers not fulfilling this duty to be good?" — "The petition of the child," he was given in answer. "Just look at me," he continued, "and take to heart what I say: the petition of the child, if it comes from a pure, child-like heart, will not only be heard, but also yielded to."

Bonhardt: "If that were so, the human would have fortune in his power, and hardship and sorrow could not reside with him."

Clergyman: "The human has his fortune in his hands; but he does not use and enjoy it, but instead throws it away and chooses in its place hardship and sorrow."

Bonhardt: "I cannot believe that. If you speak the truth over everything, here you go too far, here you place the human at a height which he can at most reach in the idea, but in practical life never achieve."

Clergyman: "He must be able to achieve it, otherwise all is closed to him by which he would be capable of perceiving the love of God. The first need of the human is to nourish himself, hence this petition is also the first which he sends with fervour to the father; and as true as the sun shines, as true as God's spirit wafts through all of creation, just as true will this petition be granted if it is directed with sincere heart and with trust to the father. The human must learn to recognise the hand of God, this is the first task, if he wants to separate himself from the animal and place himself in the class of rational beings who are capable of setting themselves the highest goal, knowledge of God."

Bonhardt: "If this were so, why then so much poverty? If the petition already sufficed, you would though see tests of such an effect and interest in it."

Clergyman: "This objection is unfortunately not without cause. When you consider humans, they seem like a herd without shepherd and lord. But on whom lies the fault? On the father or the children? The father is an eternal fountain of love. He has placed no requirement on the creature to approach him as himself and express his wishes. Where do you see this simple requirement fulfilled? Where do you see unconditional trust? Nowhere, nowhere I say; you gift and hand over your fate to protection, to cleverness, to cunning, to blind accident, and you hope of the eternal goodness, if it is indeed capable of achieving something, that it will serve our idols and not disgrace them."

Bonhardt: "To me it is as if I were hearing myself speaking in a dream. Will I ever awake to certainty?"

Clergyman: "God has given himself to us through his spirit. He is the kindly father who gives the children already at their birth the interest on their inheritance. Someone who does not collect the interest or is too idle to approach the father and to say, 'Give me what you put aside for me', has he a right to lament his fate if misfortune and hardship strike him? All is given, we may just ask and take and thank the eternal God."

Bonhardt: "If this is well founded, then it is a fortune to be penniless, by contrast a misfortune to be rich."

Clergyman: "The greatest wealth is the consciousness of standing under the care of a kindly, rich father who, elevated above worldly circumstances, lets come to us what avails us, and on the other hand protects us from hardship and misfortune."

Bonhardt: "You are expressing views in which unceasing sources of life are contained which, if they can be revealed, would have to transform the world into a paradise."

Clergyman: "The sources flow evermore and only must not be revealed; our affair is to seek their outflow and to draw from them. Certainly this seeking is subject to a few conditions which not everybody has the courage to fulfil. Three realms are given to us, for eye, ear, and feeling. The eye feasts in the outer shimmer, delights in the wealth of colours and forms and compares the most diverse relationships. The ear hears sound, tone, and word and gives us the ability to gain recognition for our ego through expressed will. Feeling is the basis and the law of life. Whoever has made himself capable of feeling the relationships of forms and colours, of words and concepts, has arrived in the sanctum, is in the quiet chamber into which Christ sends his adherents, is at the altar where all for which we pray bears the granting within itself. The world of forms changes and passes in time. The language of the mouth disperses in the air. The activity of feeling moves in the primitive matter of life and knows no change other than to make itself ever more perfect. This is in the most incomplete outlines the foundation of all teachings which occupy themselves with God and immortality. The pure knowledge of feeling was the goldmine of the old wise men, was the cube of the Pythagorean number doctrine, in a word, the mystery of all societies which set pure spiritual knowledge as the goal of their striving. Here there is no miracle, no mysticism, no, the free operation of nature founded on action and reaction. The feelings say: give us this day our daily bread, and God, the eternal love, gives, touched by this feeling, all which the creature desires. But enough of this! Let us stride on to the sixth petition."

Bonhardt, as if waking from a dream, said, "I should not have hindered you in the unfolding of your views; only I must ask you to begrudge me the time to think once more about what I have heard so that it can take root in me." The clergyman himself found it appropriate and replied, "After the meal there will yet be opportunity." The midday meal arrived; after they had fed themselves, they moved outside, and when they found themselves alone on a field path, the clergyman began.

"*Sixth petition*: And forgive us our debts, as we forgive our debtors.

In this petition a deeply shocking earnesty reigns. It expresses how close the human stands to God and God to the human. Here the identity between God and human is stated in the most indubitable way. In this petition it becomes obvious that God and man, even if not with respect to greatness, but by nature are one, must be one. Forgive me, as I forgive means to subject yourself to the eternal law of the father unconditionally in that you undertake to be like he is.

I leave it to you to analyse the content of this petition in its multifarious connections and add only that in it the law of the Old and New Testaments unite, and when God says to Moses, to the perverse I am a perverse God*; nothing more and noth-

---

*   [Tr.: cf. Psalms 18:26: With the pure thou wilt shew thyself pure; and with the froward thou wilt shew thyself froward.]

ing less is being said than: forgive us our debts, as we forgive our debtors.

Seventh petition: And lead us not into temptation, but deliver us from evil.

Here the prayer again becomes practical, where we entreat the father who gives us our daily bread to distance from us all temptation and evil. We find in the granting of this petition once again opportunity to test the impact of God on the course of our fates and to recognise the immediate vicinity of his spirit. When we turn ourselves with complete trust to the outpoured original power, the enticing hook is taken from every temptation, and that oppressive feeling which tends to consist of discontentment, unfulfilled wishes, of envy and ambition, poverty and illness, cannot win a place in us because the evil itself does not appear as evil, but rather as a test of our powers.

Many think two petitions are contained in one here; only, if we consider it precisely, they cannot be separated because every temptation is an evil and every evil is a temptation.

The greatest evil for the human is false doctrine, which under glistening forms and principles not only holds its listeners back in the darkness, but leads them into the abyss. Humans like to entertain false doctrine because it flatters their senses, prejudices, and thoughts and admits dominance. In this respect they are their own seducers and enemies, and fall, if they do not steadfastly fight, in shameful slavery where they fade away under the oppression of their own egos.

For thine is the kingdom, and the power, and the glory, for ever. Amen.

Either this closing sentence is true or it is not. When you consider humans, the latter seems to be the case; but when we turn our eyes to creation, the former forcibly imposes itself. An immutable law reigns through nature which the human recognises whilst he abandons himself to changeability and fleeting mood. Hence the kingdom remains closed to him, the outflows of the eternal power become empty names, and the pip which shall sprout shoots and fruits of the knowledge of God and his glory disintegrates into dust like the seed in poor soil.

So much for the Lord's Prayer. It is, although given in time, far from any arbitrariness. The doctrine which it expresses in the form of petitions is grounded deep in the nature of God and of humanity and allows no other interpretation than that which it expresses according to its sense. If you possess the courage and power to seek practical proof, you will arrive safely at your goal; but if you want to obtain certainty through scientific investigations, then you will entangle yourself all the more firmly until finally it becomes impossible for you to tear off your self-imposed bonds."

Bonhardt gave his word to remain brave and persistent. "What can the human", he asked, "wish for that is more beautiful and higher than to unite with God and to feel his effect on our life naturally. I thank you like a son does his father, for you have gifted me a new life."

The clergyman assured him of his unselfish joy, with the remark that it was the most beautiful reward of his life to reveal truths which he had construed as infallible. "If humans wanted to accept it," he said, "I would like to dedicate myself to teaching everything which could lead them through life; but it is as if hell had closed their minds, so obdurate and stubborn they are, from accepting the doctrine and grounding their fortunes on it. They prefer to outdo each other in complaining, instead of connecting themselves with God in accordance with their sublime calling, and using understanding and reason for what it is intended for, for knowledge of God and freedom of life. But let us leave that, it is enough if we find ourselves and strive to produce in ourselves the ideal of human nature so far as it stands within our powers. Humanity has never entirely lost itself, always representatives of its higher destiny are found; we want to follow these few, even if unrecognised by the multitude, and to strive to realise in ourselves that ancient nobility which is granted to all who receive the authority through the spirit."

The time of parting came. Bonhardt asked, "When will I see you again?" The clergyman replied, "In four weeks I will be coming to Hamburg and will seek to arrange it to spend a few hours of the day in your company." They parted, Bonhardt full of eagerness to reinforce in himself what he had heard, the clergyman in the happy prospect of having drawn someone earnestly seeking from the current of ruin.

***

5. Practical Use

It was swirling in Bonhardt's head as if he had come from pitch darkness into the light of day. Is it possible, he said to himself, to exercise for years in all subjects of thought and not notice the most necessary, the nearest thing? But surely for me, that I have been brought to the realisation! I will not spend the rest of the days of my life with useless brooding. Eternity has opened up before me, in it I must seek the fruits of my diligence.

He made the effort to find confirmation of the received doctrine in everyday life and carried out investigations to this end amongst the poorer classes. He did not find clean examples anywhere, but clear traces of a higher blessing; for in families where only some trust in God resided there was no humiliating begging, no complete poverty, by comparison in houses where this trust was lacking there reigned greed, pushiness, dishonesty, strife, envy, and hate, often with complete lack of nourishment. Are such proofs sufficient, he asked himself, to build a theory upon and to recognise the hand of God irrefutably? He continued his observations and finally came to the point where he regretted being rich and not being able to make the attempt using himself. Give them their daily bread, I must pray, and am excluded from getting closer in this way to God.

Thousands of ideas went around in his head. Often he had already half decided to renounce his wealth in order to get to know more certainly the immediacy of God; then doubt over the truth and possibility of such an effect again imposed itself on him. He then said to himself, in what way would humans have earned such a benefit? What advantage does he have over the animal which must also seek its nourishment with limited means? Would such a contact not be a miracle? Can there be miracles? I find no point on which this new doctrine is to be fortified with some confidence.

The human raises himself above the animal through his language. If special phenomena appear, they must be effected through that. But how? And why? — From where does the human have language? From God is the answer. God must accordingly possess language just as well, indeed yet more perfectly than the human, otherwise the latter could not also have it. God speaks and the human speaks, thus it is to be assumed that God and human can make themselves mutually comprehensible. Is there perhaps in language an electrical power by which one ego touches another and sets itself into operation? If that were so, then the miracles stop and the matter would have to be considered to be a natural interaction like we see frequently in nature.

But how does the language of God get through to the human? Through what channels? With what organs can the human hear it and return it to God? Through feeling, the clergyman says. The inner organs are withdrawn from the external world and can only feel the inner-being; a clear feeling, however, is raised to an idea, becomes word and thought and the indisputable possession of those who are conscious of it themselves. If we win the ability to feel letters, syllables, words, and finally sentences, then God's spirit will be connected to this feeling, will take it up in itself and grant in reaction, which must follow by necessity, the offering of the content of the expressed prayer.

Are such conclusions right? Are they to be built on it with certainty? Or are they like those sentences and premises which you so often used in school to unite the most heterogeneous things with one another? I believe not. External nature delivers phenomena of action and reaction which astonish us. It is therefore not superstitious when you say: behind the visible powers are yet others which have their peculiar, perhaps even more decisive activity.

Everything in nature rests on inflow and outflow, on action and reaction. The rays of the sun penetrate into the soil and grass and herbs arise. The wind rebounds from the cliffs. Light increases in reflection. Sound and tone echoes from mountains and walls. The echo gives back the spoken word distinctly. In the mirror the portrait of the one looking in is shown with all their contours. While the entirety of visible nature is in effective activity, should life, thought, free will, and the noblest feelings be damned to idle at rest, to inert watching? No, there is a higher, I would like to say, a divine doctrine which penetrates into the spirit of creation and espies there the basic causes of all actions. Action does not stop at the bounds of our senses. Nature has an inner spirit, a positive power which imparts to it, like alcohol to wine, life to the body, thought to the human, the essential dignity.

Give us this day our daily bread, so the human should learn to pray in his feelings, then he will receive it, my teacher says. Where one wants to be electrified, be shocked by electrical sparks, he touches the machine and the sparks spray. Since this is true, no rational law argues against it. The visible electrifier machine must, when I touch it, give me sparks; can a living electricity not just as much provide for me both the daily bread and/or the means for it? Visible electricity stands more deeply than the electricity of life, and therefore it can well give me sparks, but no daily bread. It is rationally adjudged when you say higher powers work stronger than the lower, as if you wanted to claim lower powers work for evermore, higher powers though not.

He abandoned himself for several days to such meditations without considering the subsequent petitions. To investigate inflow and outflow, action and reaction in all its ramifications was for the time being his main task, and he obtained a skill at analysing these two essential components so that he did not see any dividing wall anymore between the sensory and the extrasensory, and to him everything appeared to be a necessary step ladder on which, from the deepest to the highest, and from the highest to the deepest, without interruption, without mysticism, without coarse naturalism and fanatical super-naturalism, the initiate can obtain the ability to ascend on the simple path of nature.

Where am I getting to?, he asked finally. Am I a different person, or has the nature of the thing changed? Where I previously saw mystical darkness, I see distinct traces of pure natural laws to which you dedicate yourself and on which you can attain the ways described by them to the knowledge of God.

After fifteen days of incessant contemplation, he said, I am clear on the matter theoretically, the practice must just lead me to the secure standpoint. He continued on, after he had constrained himself calmly for a few days and collected himself again, to the sixth petition on which the clergyman had placed such a great weight.

And forgive us our debts, as we forgive our debtors.

We are like God and God like us! Is that possible! Can we achieve the perfection of God and can God descend to the weakness of the human?

There lies a chain of ideas in these words which, although linked, the human mind does not know how to connect. Forgive us our debts, as we forgive our debtors. — Are both phrases so similar that you can call them purely identical? God forgives, as we forgive; we forgive, as God forgives. Is such a forgiving necessary and required by the matter? What does it mean to forgive? If we forgive a debtor who does not pay us at all or only slowly, is it understood by that to remit the debt? One seems to have incorrectly interpreted the expression to forgive — forgiving is not remitting. To not pursue a debtor, but to forgive him, does not yet say relinquish what was lent, to gift it to him. But if we do not gift and remit, God will also not gift and remit what we owe. As strict as we are towards others, he will be towards us. The petition retains its earnestness whichever way we look at it.

What do humans owe towards each other? Good nature, and since they are the children of one father, brotherly love. They owe each other leaving to each his own and, if someone receives something from another, replacing it again. But if they remain bad-natured, loveless, and greedy, what then?

What do we owe God? Love, thankfulness, and child-like trust. But if we are loveless, unthankful, and stubborn, what then?

The human may, so it seems, instruct the ignorant, show the errant the way, and remind the dilatory of their duty. Or would this be an encroachment on the eternal laws? Does not

God also remind, admonish, and instruct those who forget what they owe him? Will he remit the sins of every sinner, even if he does not draw near him? Such contends with the nature of the matter. Anyone who distances himself from the father will abandon himself to his own fate, and there can only be talk of forgiveness if he returns with the intention of fulfilling his duties. The extent to which his debts are to be remitted will depend absolutely on the manner of his return and his means. Thus it may also be amongst humans; if they forget their debts and go away, we should indeed not hate them, but our claims and their obligations are not lifted, and with every opportunity we may instruct those errant ones and remind them of their commitment without injuring the law of love.

But when is admonishing not loveless? What mortal is capable of finding the right boundary where a reprimand does not harm and increase the obduracy of the debtor? Forgive us our debts, as we forgive our debtors remains with the most exact analysis a petition which must attune us, if we stand so near to God, for evermore to the earnestness and to the contemplation of our sublime calling. For this reason there follows also in the seventh petition the honest confession that we feel without powers from above incapable of the fulfillment of our duties and are only through spiritual enlightenment in a position to find the right way.

And lead us not into temptation, but deliver us from evil.

The one whom temptation does not approach is free from evil, for the greatest evil is temptation. The greatest tempter of the human, however, is himself with his desires, wishes, and plans. He would like to possess everything, know everything, do and enjoy everything. Because of the seemingly utterly necessary relaxations and activities, he finds no time for his true calling, to think for himself, and fritters away his life in dreamt-up activities for human welfare; for that reason you guard yourself from yourself more than from all other seductions; you test, before you undertake something, whether it is decided from pure intention to do good things, or merely to indulge your desires, weaknesses, and whims; then the certainty is obtained to avoid all temptations and deceptions.

Deliver us from evil is the conclusion of the petition and of the prayer, and truly, if this petition is fulfilled, then nothing more remains for the human to wish for. Father! Deliver me from the darkness in which I languish; deliver me from this greatest of evils so that I obtain the ability to inquire into your names, recognise your will, and perceive the effect of your spirit on me.

For thine is the kingdom, and the power, and the glory, for ever. Amen.

So it is, so must it be, since the creation, his house, his clothes, I would like to say his body, are through his spirit in motion and action steadfast, firm, and eternal.

I possess the doctrine, he said after he had read through the last pages of his journal, but I am like one who knows farming from books, but has never concerned himself practically about it and worked in it. You must learn to recognise the hand of God, otherwise you are not the son, but rather a lost creature who has no hope, no support, and no confidence. But how can I achieve this knowledge, since I possess everything which I should have first received from him? My wealth is my misfortune, he continued in embarrassment; it hinders me from approaching the father and bringing him my thanks.

Tormented by these thoughts, he fell into a sort of pensiveness which struck everything around him. Frequently he even said to himself, affluence is a gift of God of which you must not dispose without offending the giver. Another time, however, he said, if I did not pluck from the tree which my father left behind for me, instead tasting the fruits of another, can that surely be a sacrilege? To forego for ten years the enjoyment of my wealth does not mean to throw it away, but rather to make myself more able to administer and use it expediently. Ten years, he said aloud, of dining at the table of the eternal father would connect me with him in such a way that a separation would not be thinkable anymore and the relationship of a father to the son would be fashioned in the most indubitable way.

In such a way he philosophised often for hours and finally resolved to forgo the enjoyment of his wealth for ten years in order to make the certain test of in what connection the human stood to God and God to the human.

When the clergyman came to Hamburg, he had already initiated everything for his plan, and was transferring to him the power to administer his wealth and the naming of a legal guardian. "I cannot do anything else," he said when the clergyman sought to divert him from his plan; "I must convince myself through experience whether your doctrine is well-grounded and I am a worthy student. I will go to a foreign city where nobody knows me. Do not reveal to anyone the cause of my departure either. I would not like others to find fault with me or even call me a second Diogenes*. My intention is only to come to the truth in a practical way; this they would not believe and take offence at. Allow me to stay with you for a few months in order to strengthen myself in the new doctrine and obtain courage to face up to the unavoidable temptations."

He moved to his friend's place. After two months he left, equipped with only a little cash in order to soon be required to seek that source from which he was resolved to draw his life's needs in future.

For ten years he remained away from his home town without anyone learning anything about him. Even the clergyman was in ignorance of his fate and was often worried when he reflected on how easily enthusiasm and excited fantasy are suited for misguiding humans into error. Finally after ten years a carriage stopped before his house in the afternoon. A man along with a woman and two children climbed out. The clergyman on hearing the rattling hurried to the window, saw the travellers, but yet had no inkling of the vicinity of his friend. The latter rushed up the steps, embraced the clergyman, while he cried out, "Welcome teacher and friend!" The clergyman could not believe his eyes, and asked, "Are you really the one?" "I am," Bonhardt answered, "and have come to thank you and to tell you that I have gotten to know God's hand, his name, his kingdom, and his heaven, and found that without the nearness of the eternal and without the knowledge of his spirit no salvation, no confidence, and no belief is possible." The clergyman hurried to the front of the house

---

*   [Tr.: Diogenes (c. 400 – c. 325 B.C.E) was a Greek ascetic philosopher, one of the Cynics, who emphasised self-sufficiency and behaving naturally.]

and asked the woman and children to likewise enter. They followed him, and arriving in the room the woman said, "Take me on as kindly as you formerly did my husband, and I will call myself your student with honest gratitude." Bonhardt continued, "She is your student, she lives in the spirit of your doctrine and has felt like me how secure one walks under the eyes of the father. I parted from you without means, now you see me again rich in earthly goods and yet blessed by the fortune of the love of a wife and children who provide me with all the joys of life which are capable of being enjoyed by mortals. Rejoice with me, and if the feeling of having established something good can refresh a heart, then delight in the thought of having led me from the darkness to the most blessed light, and from confusion to the highest fortune."

Bonhardt spent a few days with his friend, then he went to Hamburg to order his affairs and to take over the administration of his wealth again. After he had ordered everything, he said, while he gave an account of the events of his ten year test to his friend, "I would not advise anyone else to follow my example. Often I ended up in situations where I considered myself lost; but like a miracle strength and salvation came. Without persistence you do not obtain eternal goods; but anyone who perseveres is certain of the reward."

***

Part 2: The Canonical Law

1. The Letter

Bonhardt had, after he had straightened out his money affairs, bought a house, and had already been living for three years in a private capacity, indeed on his gleaming but respectable feet. Every man of culture who pays tribute only to some extent to a higher philosophy than the usual dilemmatic one has access with it; and thus it happened that he saw once and often several times a week a circle of friends about himself who conversed over everything which was concerning human destiny and the freedom of spirit, and often produced extremely instructive discussions. Bonhardt, to whom on account of not only his learned education, but principally the experiences made in this respect, a decisive predominance was given, had to take over the office of adjudicator in order to prevent any disagreements arising with the diversity of views. In this way a sort of club developed in his house for which nothing was lacking but the tendency to put things to paper systematically and to declare a constitution. Against that, however, Bonhardt was on his guard. "We are", he said, "assembling as friends and need no other constitution than the earnest will to instruct each other mutually, to respect and to love as befits all men."

It had gone on like that for two years when a new object made demands on their activity. *The Life of Jesus, Critically Examined* by David Friedrich Strauss* had appeared in the bookshops and had been read widely in many different ways

---

*   [Tr.: first published in German in 1835, and translated into English in 1848 by George Eliot.]

with the strangest judgements, sometimes completely damned, sometimes praised to the heavens. It could not fail that such a book must excite a great furore in a company which made higher philosophy the topic of its conversations. All views seemed to have changed, mythology became the keyword with most when they found no other excuse anymore. Bonhardt himself, whose office as adjudicator often required him to speak about it, could, irrespective of him not agreeing with the content of the book, do no damage to the conclusiveness of it. In such embarrassment he said, "We are too weak to ascend this mountain; I must seek help where it alone is to be found, with the man who has already drawn me out of the darkness once before." He wrote the next day to his friend and asked him to provide him a safe guide for judging the named book, and to tell him absolutely on what basic law the content of the Bible rests. After a few days he received the following answer.

Dear friend!

The Life of Jesus, Critically Illuminated* by D.F. Strauss is a book which preferably should never have been published. In order to make this clear to your eyes, allow me to depart from the usual form of a letter and to present to you my views in the way of paragraphs.

1.

If belief has some worth and is capable of drawing the human to the divine, then it is extremely incorrect to rob him of this fortune and to plunge him almost with violence from eternity into the rough temporal world. You must wonder how the present-day clergy, whose indispensable duty it would be to awaken, to promote, and to support belief, may place their doubt so publicly on show and thereby lose their high calling's most precious and securest adornment. Such sorts of books as the present one, even if they are also based on truth, are not suited for the masses, all the less so if their content rests on false ideas and premises which

---

*   [Tr.: the incorrect title is in the original German.]

also bear not a grain of the pure knowledge of God and true theology in themselves.

2.

Dr Strauss has after many citations and analyses of naturalism, rationalism, and supernaturalism set up a fourth, myth, as an infallible means of interpreting the Bible, and suggests by that to be able to explain all the events and miracles of the Old and New Testaments. Naturalism, as is well-known to you, wants to look at everything in natural ways, and what deviates from that is to it fabrication and lies. Rationalism denies no event, but models them after the laws of reason, pronounces to be sleight of hand or deception that which does not fit into its logic, adds, throws away, and recomposes for as long as until it agrees with the laws of thinking suited to academia. Supernaturalism is all literal truth, and the more miraculous, the better, because in the degree of miraculousness of a thing the meritoriousness of the belief also grows. What does mythology do?, you might ask. It considers, according to Dr Strauss's definition, the core of the phenomena and the stories to be the truth, but claims that the incomprehensible and miraculous has been added through the telling by following generations. This strangeness and wondrousness is detached from the core and gives according to Strauss's view the pure truth.

3.

I spoke above about false premises on which the content of the book rests, and it is difficult to comprehend how the weakness of his mythological foundations could have escaped the author and his adherents. Stripping something of its attached telling is almost the same as if we made a thing by virtue of reason suited for academia through additions and omissions. Such a mythological process is rationalism under a different form. Since now Dr Strauss describes rationalism as being insufficient, he has given judgement himself over his own work. Neither naturalism, rationalism, supernaturalism, nor myths are sufficient to explain the spirit of the Bible, there must be yet a fifth thing which encompasses it both in its entire extent and as history, morals, and divine doctrine; then if it is confirmed by putting it to the test, all parties can approach one another and work to one goal with united powers.

4.

In order to go to work logically with a thing of such importance as the present theological crisis, one must investigate what interest humans take in such disputes; whether they are participating in them, and which of their wishes, hopes, and needs are endangered. The answer is close by. The investigation delivers with any human child a quick and certain result. The human wants to live. To preserve his life, to lengthen it, to strengthen it, to guide it beyond the grave, is an urge which lies deep in every heart; and if sacred books shall achieve anything, they must contribute to the realisation of this eternal drive; if writers venture in the interpretation of the named books, they must seek in them this kernel, strive to place it before the eyes of the masses in an ever clearer manner so that that which previously was only suspicion, wish, and hope becomes belief and finally certainty.

5.

Immortality is the human's goal and desire, and if it is to be attained, his most sacred calling. The human thinks with horror of death. He devotes himself with delight to the hope of immortality. He sees the other side of the grave as his home, his place of refuge from the storms of time, the land of his most blissful presentiments, the satisfaction of his innermost wishes, in short, calm and peacefulness, bound with the greatest freedom of the will. With what name should you describe this state of the soul of the human? Where is a power found which keeps the balance with the invincible drive, the love for life? And is it perhaps reprehensible to wish for, to hope for, and finally to believe in that which we recognise as the highest, have to recognise as necessary by laws of nature? It is to be censured if, in order to arrive at certainty, we toil the way the poor man toils who preserves his family from starvation through hard work? Dying is gruesome, and the more we learn to comprehend the fullness of life, the more unbearable is the idea of an eternal death. Take from the man of integrity the prospect of immortality, and all the charms of life vanish, his nobility of mind becomes a craftsmanlike tribute without reward, without confidence and strengthening; he no longer knows how to array any weapon against misfortune, but in good fortune he becomes dizzy because the standpoint of his life has shifted. The idea of immortality makes the human into the human, the belief in it is to him, if he shall remain human and not turn into an animal, as necessary a requirement as food and drink is for the body.

6.

We have come to the point where a requirement of nature instructs us and prescribes laws. For this reason there must be life laws which stand under this necessity and show the means to the satisfaction of that requirement. Where now are such laws? Perhaps in a science? Certainly not. Can reason, on which every science rests, make abstract conclusions in order to satisfy us in this? Just as little. Indeed the scholars believe reason itself is the immortal part, and will, when the decision nears, already take care of itself; but they forget that in sleep, in feverish illnesses and more with a glass of wine, reason knows nothing more of them and they nothing more of reason. Or perhaps they believe that in death, in the eternal sleep, reason will again awaken and be active with renewed power? Does that not sound like reasoning in the following way? — The fountain, with appropriate water pressure, leaps high — if the pressure is weak, it does not leap as high — but if you shall take away the water and break the pipes, it will then leap quite high.

7.

We see how unfruitful the regions touched on are for the end goal of our desires. We must strike a new path in order to still the yearning of our hearts. Supernaturalism makes belief into the indispensable condition, but in a way which opposes the claims of the free will. We also make belief the foundation to arriving at better knowing. It turns out accordingly that there are two sorts of belief which, since only one leads to the right path, must be distinguished necessarily by specific features. Supernaturalism believes in a kingdom of grace where one gives one person a lot, the other little, the third nothing at all, but covers the fourth with every abundance. Freedom of will is to it a sacrilege because everything which God gives happens from special favour. He considers these ones in the way the kings of the earth do, who have their favourites while the others go away empty handed. God is to them indeed father, but such a one who makes unequal parts and withholds and hands out capriciously. It is superfluous to speak further about it here. True belief must not lose the freedom, it must insist on knowledge and must never be permitted to despair in its appropriation, even if it still lies so far away.

8.

Knowledge must come to us if we shall be placated over our destiny. Knowledge must be able to be granted to us if the human shall not be cut short by the creator who set everything in perfection. True knowledge does without temporal knowledge, it penetrates into eternity and looks around there for what share the human has in it.

9.

Immortality exists. It is the goal of humanity, but also at the same time the greatest miracle of creation. I call it a miracle because it contradicts the course of nature, even if only seemingly, and cannot be comprehended and analysed with the usual powers of thought. The scholars themselves believe in immortality, in the greatest miracle, but lesser ones consider it impossible. They play with the axle of the wheel, the surrounding area and the spokes they deny. Anyone who does not believe in spiritual effectiveness also does not believe, even if he reinforces it with oaths, in immortality. Immortality, as the greatest miracle, in addition to all the Biblical phenomena which is inexplicable to us, bases itself on higher laws of nature, knowledge of which in our days is no longer sought, but rather denied as a limitation of an immature age.

10.

We call the Bible holy scripture. Holy is to humanity that which encompasses its most intimate wishes and hopes. There is nothing higher for it that the consciousness of an immortal life. The Bible must for this reason, if it should prove its worth as a holy book, touch on these interests and indicate the path to their satisfaction. Already from this point of view it can be interpreted neither naturally, rationally, supernaturally, nor mythically. — It is the law of life, symbolised by historically symbolic phenomena which make us attentive to the spirit of the law in order to come through practical exercise to a like stage.

11.

The Bible as law is at the same time history. From law and history arise morals. The Bible must be considered according to these in a threefold direction if we want to survey the whole and take into ourselves the multifarious points of light which are contained in it. The history is evidence of the effectiveness of the law, the morals become through history and law the necessary condition because the first social arrangements and virtues can be touched, but the law cannot be recognised and fulfilled without morals.

12.

It is the law which lies between rationalism and supernaturalism and indicates to us the spirit of the Bible. It goes without saying that here there is no talk of any arbitrary law like we see in everyday life and learn by memory, here it is essentially laws of nature which are unalterable and eternal, like the laws of harmony, of the colours, of gravity and spherical motion. Here we should get to know the interaction between matter and spirit, between form and God, between striving for freedom and its possession. It is a task of practical nature for whose solving we possess the capability, but without practice will not attain even with the most brilliant powers of mind.

13.

The wise ones of earlier ages had drawn up a canon in which the perfections of human nature were brought together. Procreation, growth in the mother's body, birth, physical thriving, aptitude, education and instruction, life and death were taken into consideration, and the closer a human came to this ideal, to the canonical law, the more blessed he felt and praised God who had already decided from eternity to reveal his glory, his light, and his word in humanity and had chosen him for his son.

14.

The canon posits three sorts of children of God:
1. such who appear without physical parents through action of the divine spirit on soft earth which forms a uterus;
2. those who are born through a woman without admixture of the man;
3. children of natural parents who through themselves and the power of the spirit produce the messiah within themselves and rise through the rebirth to be sons of God.

The Bible delivers us examples of all three sorts and names them, in distinction to the common children of humanity, children of God. Around the last assemble the communities which hope to take part through the belief in the canonical law in the promises which the children of God see fulfilled already in the here and now. In such a way a church, a kingdom of God, forms which is far from dark dogma, obeying only the higher laws of nature, can unite us all in itself and lead us to immortality.

15.

Those spiritual heroes formed their canon, their ideals not for this visible world, but rather for a higher world, for the kingdom of the angels and saints. They did not recognise any empty, inanimate space in creation. From the deepest to the highest they saw an uninterrupted hierarchy whose beginning and end indeed reached into eternity, but nevertheless moving under unalterable laws can be investigated and recognised. They said God, who founded a stronghold between the waters and over the water, has separated all the basic powers of his creation by strongholds and prescribed for them the unescapable paths of their efficacy. In the water the human, on dry land the fish cannot come to be and live. Everything has its sphere which it is dependent upon and any matter can serve as procreative receptacle for living species. Deep under the earth, even in rocks where the limited understanding of humans sees no possibility of an effect of light, a breathing in of air, a movement, nor a means of nourishment, living species of animal are found. In matter, in the roughest, hardest matter visible to us, the miracle of life begins and only ends in the sea of light of the almighty whose animating brilliance surrounds all world systems. We see earth and water inhabited by living creatures; do we have a reason to conclude that death reigns in the regions of air and light? Earth and water are separated by a stronghold, likewise water and air. To an incalculable extent the latter floats over the earth, and is separated by a secure stronghold of the circle of light, like the air from water and the water from the earth. Thus circles form on circles, strongholds on strongholds up to the highest, to the inner sanctum of God where the circles of light of all the heavenly bodies move, flow into one another, and connect in this way the creation to an immeasurable whole. In those purer elements, before the earth was populated, creatures were already present which had formed out of the purest ether and were free from the pressure of mortality, open only to the higher influences and accepting amongst themselves in jubilation the saints of God who free themselves from dust.

16.

The Bible mentions one more kingdom which strives against the kingdom of light and hinders its expansion, the kingdom of darkness, hell. It was not created by God, but rather produced by the sins which arose from free will, the highest good of perfect creatures. Free will can choose, good or evil, life or death. Sins are accordingly the consequence of the most sublime feature of rational beings, because only these can decide to turn from the eternal laws to a self-described path. Angels have fallen, humans have fallen and the kingdom of darkness is becoming ever greater until someday a new world order shall occur and the word of God shall be recognised again amongst humanity and shall be heard through all lands.

17.

These few lines are the outline of the Bible. Anyone who crosses out just one line has destroyed the Bible. They are the pillars of the Old and New Testaments, of which none may be removed without collapsing the whole into rubble. They are the law of which Christ himself said, anyone who dissolves the least of it is condemned to the eternal fire*. What would the holy scripture be without Adam, the first born; the son of God blinded by Satan? Without him, the father of a numerous progeny dedicated to God? What would it be without Moses and the prophets? What without the spiritual power of Christ, with which he healed illnesses and commanded storms? Without his wisdom, with which he connected with the father and saw unveiled everything which was and will be? It would be the most incomplete book which we would have inherited from antiquity; a chaos of teachings and stories from which nobody could draw salvation nor light. Any impartial person will see the inadmissibility of even only the slightest reform of the Bible and be forced either to completely deny it or to acknowledge it in its entirety.

18.

All that has been said up to now is noble and sublime and suited to familiarising us with eternity, but the essential proof of immortality is still lacking. Since I am convinced that you will find this yourself, or have already found it, I will remain silent on it and only add

---

*   [Tr.: cf. Mark 9:43–48, Matthew 5:22, Matthew 18:8.]

that the human can rise through it to the uppermost level and himself found his future life in the brilliance of the eternal majesty.

Take what I have written as tested proof. Some of it will indeed appear foreign to you, but time and calm contemplation will guide you to conviction. Tearing down is easy, hence be on your guard for error, as the evil whose consequences are only made good again slowly. Be well and accept my assurance of unwavering love and friendship.

Bonhardt read the letter and was so surprised by the content that he fell into doubt over the impression which it would make on his friends. He let eight days pass before he notified them of the receipt of it, and only after they had urged him to admonish his teacher and ask him for an answer had he revealed the document and said, "Here is the explanation; only the principles contained in it deviate so much from all previous Bible interpretations that I bore reservations about sharing it with you. But in the conviction your calm minds and your love of truth will hold you back from premature judgements, I want to suppress my doubt and entreat you to listen to the answer with appropriate attentiveness.

He read the letter aloud slowly and with the expression which the importance of the content demanded. Already during the reading the mood of the company was expressing itself, but at the paragraphs over immortality several gave audible indications of their liking. After the last paragraphs a silence reigned, as if they wanted to count the beats of their hearts. Bonhardt had read to the end and heard no sound. A spontaneous astonishment seemed to have gripped everyone. Finally a member of the company, a clergyman, interrupted the silence and said, "I admire this writing in a way I have never admired anything else. Its content allocates to the Bible the standpoint which it deserves in that he places it at the peak of all knowledge and capability." A doctor, also member of the company, said, "The man who wrote this letter makes little trouble; despising the palliative, he goes to the root of the matter and proves that it must be so." A third continued, "It is the spirit of the Bible which speaks spirit-like from the writing and puts us to the test of whether we want to deny it or believe it with all its puzzles and miracles." A fifth praised the paragraphs which spoke about immortality. A sixth felt fortunate to be able to make himself worthy of membership of the children of God. A jurist who would have long since liked to have spoken concurred with the above using the following words, "The letter writer discusses heaven and hell, earth and stars, angels and the devil with a certainty like the way we, when looking at a map, speak of foreign lands. Only I must confess his views are so bold that I doubt I am able to follow him."

"Why should we not follow him?", one of the members replied. "Humans can do much when they possess courage; this we must not lack since we are men. Only I must ask to not consider it the end of the matter with the hearing of the letter. No, the subject must be pondered, be carefully investigated, and be analysed in its basic components; hence I am suggesting the discussion and investigation in our meetings of one paragraph after the other, and where we feel ourselves too weak to find the truth, asking our friend Bonhardt to come to our help with his experience."

Everybody supported this suggestion and asked Bonhardt to set specific days on which they could assemble with him to this end. He agreed in this desire and invited them, as long as it was not decided otherwise, to his place twice weekly, on Monday and Thursday evenings. They thanked him for this compliance with their will and parted, each thinking about the content of the letter in his own way.

***

2. Discussion of the Letter

First Evening

When the company had assembled on the specified evening, they expressed the wish to hear once more the first paragraph* of the letter. Bonhardt read it aloud and invited the members to express their views over it. The jurist spoke first and gave of himself in the following way.

"The paragraph just read makes it a duty of the clergy to awaken, promote, and support belief. Now it is to be asked whether blind belief or rational belief is to be understood by that. In the first case I cannot give my agreement because blind faith is not consistent with the freedom of humanity. In the second case I ask for caution in how far reason is allowed to occupy itself with matters of belief."

Bonhardt responded, "Blind faith is abasing for human nature, notwithstanding which it is often indispensable. Someone who cannot rise to knowledge must content themselves with belief. But belief and knowledge, if the highest, God and eternity, is the goal of their activity, both lead to life. Belief is a feeling, and as such, if it is not suppressed by arrogance of knowing, it dominates human nature as completely as knowledge. Just as the lover must involuntarily follow the pull of his heart, the one awakened to belief also cannot withstand the urge of his disposition. Rational belief, however, is

---

* See p. 58.

like a rational marriage where the participants, excluding exceptions, never feel the fortune of marriage to its full extent."

"But if", the jurist replied, "the affinity of the lovers argues against reason?"

"Then love may", Bonhardt responded, "compensate; and truly! Its power is capable of transforming the cottage into the palace and the wasteland into paradise."

"I am vanquished," the jurist said, "and pay tribute to the feeling of belief, as of love."

Through the simile between rational marriage and rational belief the matter became clear to all, and they were pleased to be able to imagine clearly under such a simple image what is not achieved by many a book having respect to this. They considered the simile from all sides, sought to investigate the agreement in every respect, and came to the result that, if belief is present as feeling in human nature, nothing can be said against the claim of the first paragraph. Bonhardt said on this note, "Belief is a feeling like the urge to take a spouse. When full maturity arrives, this expresses itself. When we learn to admire God's omnipotence through the sight of creation, when we are drawn to recognise the relationship between us and the creator, be it through word, text, or own inquiry, then the urge to belief is awoken, and surely for anybody who preserves their feeling in this crisis of life; he walks with certain steps through the storms of the world and builds on the power of the eternity to which his heart is tied."

Everyone agreed with these views. Only they could not explain how belief, when it works as a living feeling in humans, could lead to such horrors as history frequently revealed. Bonhardt responded, "Precisely this proves that it reigns as feeling in us. To what extremes, to what crimes does the love of the spouse lead? Hence, when feeling enters into one's rights, reason is necessary in order to rein in the expression of the former and to keep it firmly on the track which leads us to fortune and life's aim."

"We are satisfied!", everyone called out, and Bonhardt read out the second paragraph[*]. After a short pause, a doctor of

---

[*] See p. 59.

law, rich in means and life experience, desired to speak and began as follows.

"Naturalism, rationalism, and supernaturalism are the stages of life of the greater part of humanity. I myself see in these three terms the story of my previous existence before me. Perhaps it will serve for understanding to hear of such things, hence I ask for a few moments of your attention.

I am the son of very nice, severely religious and pious parents. They made efforts to educate me in this spirit in order, as my father expressed himself, to secure me from the temptations of the world. They succeeded too, as long as I remained in their vicinity; but hardly had I escaped their supervision than I tore off the bridle of mechanically learnt principles and gave myself over, indeed without entirely throwing myself away, to the dominance of the senses. Arts and sciences, nature and religion seemed to me nothing else but means for refining the animal pleasures in order to be able to feast without interruption or slackening. I was a naturalist in the strictest sense of the word, and I pleased myself in the consciousness of drawing and of limiting God himself in the circle of sensual impressions. For many years I rushed from pleasure to pleasure, and would not have stopped had not surfeit and finally a feeling of shame over the insignificance of my life befallen me. I gave it a lot of thought and said, not the world of the senses, reason must order the course of my days, otherwise we are floating on a sea without compass and anchor. My parents had in the meantime, without having learned of my apostasy of their teachings, passed away. For the first time in a long time I thought of them again and their admonitions, only I soon noted that these were just as little to be reconciled with reason as they were to be reconciled with my previous behaviour. I remain indecisive for a long time, but finally I was compelled to give myself over to the guidance of reason and to draw from it the teachings for the future of my days. It went magnificently. Everything which I heard and saw I subjected to my critique, and came to where I imagined I was penetrating all the mist. But strangely, with the certainty of cutting up everything with the scissors of reason, the warmth of my heart died away and with it the charms of life. 'What is it?', I now asked. 'Is the human perhaps not destined to be happy? What shall help him achieve happiness if reason cannot? Reason is too cold for blissful happiness!', I cried out. It is indeed a great possession of human nature through which it grants us free will, but it is also at the same time the obedient servant of our moods and weaknesses, our desires and passions. 'Reason must turn itself to God and win his recognition,' I said to myself once in surprise. In that region it cannot degenerate and lead to any evil. Now I believed I had found the aim of a more noble activity, but soon saw I had also deceived myself in that; wherever my critical eye turned, I caught sight of meaningless forms and precepts, and the traditions of religion disintegrated into fantasy images in which I saw no connection and content. The human is a poor creature, I thought now wistfully; his best powers become dull when he wants to raise himself to the heights, to something positively sacred. In such moments I began to envy my parents their pious minds which made them so happy. If I could obtain such a disposition, I often sighed from the depths of my soul, then I would be rich and not be standing there like a blind man who has lost his guide. I spent uneasy days in this state and by and by became, without knowing it myself exactly, a pietist, or as others call it, a supernaturalist. My parents, I now said often, were right — pious belief alone leads to true happiness. From that time I connected to company which harmonised with the mood of my heart, and found at first nourishment and edification; but soon the halo vanished — the existence bound to individual sentences, the meritoriousness of blind belief became a burden to me, and I threw this staff away, without hope of finding another, with the firm resolve before me of preferring to possess nothing at all than profiting from fake gold. In this state I got to know Bonhardt, he drew me into this company and here I hope finally to obtain the standpoint which will free me from all doubts."

Everyone had listened attentively and thanked him for the story which portrayed practically in one image naturalism, rationalism, and supernaturalism. "Who will not give us a lecture on the myths brought into use by Dr Strauss?", a member of the company asked. Bonhardt suggested that since mythology is dealt with and taught everywhere, it is superfluous to speak about it here. "And yet it must", the merchant Glump said, "be spoken about in order to preserve us from misunderstandings in the course of our discussion. Hence I allow myself the question, what is mythology?"

Bonhardt: "A doctrine of the powers of the primitive spirit and of nature, typified by names and persons whom you call gods."

Glump: "Why is the term mythology not attached to the Bible?"

Bonhardt: "Because it does not personify, but considers everything which is and was and will be to be the outflow of a single power, a single God."

Glump: "But does it not have the same goal as the other?"

Bonhardt: "No different, only in simpler and more obvious forms. It is the first written book which delivers the knowledge of the creator and his spirit not in mythological, but in historical images. And hence it cannot be brought under any of the above-named rubrics, least of all into the class of mythological determinations."

Glump: "In this way every people would have a sort of Bible or divine doctrine in its mythology?"

Bonhardt: "God is eternal, is omnipresent, and hence every people must possess the means of recognising him. In our time it is only a question of where the best means is to be found, and there the safest path is shown in Christ and ancient Israel."

Glump: "I understand. Only by their form, not by their nature do humans differ in this, and under every form, or on each of the paths described by the progenitors the goal is to be reached?"

Bonhardt: "Can you conclude anything else from the eternal love and fairness of God?"

Glump: "No, truly not. Thank you for this instruction, all the more since it has cost me many a struggle when someone has sought to prove to me dictatorially that the goal is only to be achieved on one path."

All the members agreed with these words and decided to go on to the third paragraph*. It was read aloud and several voices were raised to speak about it.

The clergyman, who by virtue of his calm gift for judgement was given the lead, spoke as follows.

"The premises set up by Dr Strauss are false and must be false, otherwise we would be required to remove every higher adornment and to consider all teachings of holiness and spiritual freedom as legends. What do we possess for proof of a higher destiny if you take from us the crown of having a divine father and place human nature, like that of plants and animals, alone under the influences of visible elements? The human must come about in an unusual way, he must have experienced the unusual and the unusual is still in store for him, otherwise he is no good, in areas where you can say he is superior, to recognise the glory of God and to see it before the throne of the eternal one in renewed brilliance. Reason does not suffice to make this comprehensible, just as little as mythological images; and if you transfer completely what we have inherited from our fathers into the realm of legends and fables, then we will possess nothing at all anymore onto which intuition, hope, and belief can hold."

"So it is," Bonhardt added. "Divine truths are not demonstrable, they must be attained. Just for that reason, because Dr Strauss builds everything on speculation even his myths can only be recognised in syllogistic ways, thus it would be a waste of time to speak further about it. I put it therefore that we should close the discussion for today and not let ourselves be blinded in the feeling of a living faith, neither by naturalism, rationalism, supernaturalism, nor myth."

Everybody gave their assent and looked forward in advance to the next meeting.

Second Evening

At the appropriate hour all had gathered and after Bonhardt had brought their attention to the importance of the fourth paragraph†, he read it aloud.

---

*   See p. 59.

†   See p. 60.

"Now it's getting serious," the merchant Glump said, and he asked that they indeed go to work quite thoroughly. All were of the same view, and a magistrate member began the discussion with the following words.

"The letter writer sets about investigating what interests humans take in theological disputes, whether they participate in them, and which have endangered their wishes, hopes, and needs. He gives the answer in the name of humanity itself and expresses what everybody feels and thinks in their innermost being — the human wants to live, wants to continue his life past the grave; in this wish, yearning I would like to call it, everyone concurs and desires the conviction that they are one tribe, of one mind, and children of one and the same father."

Another used the momentary pause that occurred now, and said, "The human wants to live, this wish is written in the heart of each and we cannot rid ourselves of it by any resignation, not even by the pressure of misfortune."

A third said, "It is an innate thing about the life of humans. Sometimes we seem to pay no attention to it, but at certain times, especially in moments of danger, the love for it makes itself known in a way that we must acknowledge clearly to be the basic drive of our existence. All other needs, desires, and passions fall silent in such moments and the life drive dominates us as all-powerfully as if nothing were present in creation which had worth except for our personality. I believe if this feeling had not lost its strength through various inhibitions and doubts, humanity would have to take the standpoint where everybody found the necessity in themselves for such a highest goal which shows itself as the need to live, and to seek again the springs from which immortality flows and to open them for themselves and others."

One of the members, who did not seem entirely pleased with this talk, responded, "What our friend said about the love for one's own life may be all well and good, but to consider it to be the basic drive of our existence, to be the need which can only be satisfied by immortality, sounds so egotistical that I would not like to pass over this view unconditionally. Are there not moments when higher feelings make it our duty to put our lives at stake? Is the soldier permitted in the storm of battle to think of his life? Will the noble person who with the danger of a fire fetches a child from the flames still measure the danger against his life? The claim that love for one's own life is a need, is a law of nature, cannot find confirmation in such moments."

"You are right," Bonhardt replied; "and your remarks create the opportunity to illuminate the matter from another side too. There are moments when one's own life seems to lose worth and is considered only in respect to others. Someone who leaps into the current to rescue a drowning person does it in order to raise the prize of life. The soldier in the storm of battle heightens the feeling through the magic of honour; to stand by the one in need of help, to remain courageous in the tumult of battle are stakes in the great lottery of immortality where you may be certain of the win."

"There is accordingly a virtue", the jurist said, "which does not rest on human statutes, but rather on laws of nature?"

"Who will deny that?", Bonhardt answered.

"By what", asked another, "does true virtue distinguish itself from fake virtue?"

"Where nature commands", Bonhardt said, "there is true virtue; where convenience or public honour come into play there is fake virtue."

Everybody expressed that they were satisfied. The clergyman, however, continued. "The natural human is sacred, the worldly human is not. The former gets immortality, the latter passes into dust. Let us leave the fourth paragraph and pass on to the fifth* in order to obtain in the hearing of it new points of light to see the path to immortality." Bonhardt read. The company listened with great attentiveness and at the end each seemed to want to utter his thoughts about it. A businessman requested permission to speak and expressed the following.

"The human thinks with horror of death! He devotes himself with delight to the hope of immortality. In these two sentences is contained the quintessence and the goal of our striving, of our wishes and obligations. Fear when faced with death and yearning for life dictate the morals, and in the wildest joy sounds the warning to not let yourself sink entirely.

---

*   See p. 60.

And from that it emerges that the human must be born for the hereafter, must possess the ability to prepare himself for it just like for his worldly profession."

Another continued, "In this paragraph it is talking about not only immortality in general, but of the way in which it will appear; through it we attain the home, the place of refuge from the storms of time, the land of the most blessed intimations, the satisfaction of the innermost wishes, in short rest and contentment, bound with the highest freedom of the will and of the spirit. Such an outlook can warm our disposition and move us to a few sacrifices. Only those who know then what they receive for a reward undertake the work; but someone who puts it off until a fortune which one does not know, which has no name and at most exists in the inert gazing at an eternal glory, will never pull themselves together forcibly in order to obtain a good which is unfamiliar and undisclosed to him."

Another member responded to this talk, "I find it too daring to want to bring the state of the future life under ideas of earthly circumstances. Not the creature of dust, only the spirit can enter into eternity. Its being, however, according to all we have heard and know, is of quite different nature to the life of the senses. Accordingly an entirely new, not yet suspected state must arise if it shall correspond to the demands of the spirit in its simplicity."

Bonhardt, to whom this remark seemed to have been directed, answered, "If an entirely new, unsuspected state emerges, then we have no part in it, and the hope for immortality becomes a problem which is solvable for the whole, but for us, as a particular ego, unsolvable. Our thoughts and feelings, our hopes and desires, our beliefs and their fulfillment, our loves with all the bliss of satisfaction, all that we must take across, then the condition for a truly eternal life will be fulfilled."

"So it is, so it must be," the jurist said. "What use is the light when it flickers out? What would we have from the spirit of life if it split up again in the great sea of light? It would certainly continue to exist, but not for us, not for our joys and feelings. Everything, everything must be remain to us, even free will; as the letter writer says, must not be lacking, otherwise we become spiritual machines, serving a law which can indeed increase our life, but can also destroy it."

Several members found this remark too glaring, even, as a few expressed it, unchristian, and a general debate unwound. To many it became clear by and by that the entering into an entirely new state meant destroying our individuality, our ego, but others could not get this idea straight for a long time. Bonhardt gave his view to such doubts, that with the loss of memory our entire existence was already abrogated and we could not say in such cases anymore that we had preserved the life. He claimed furthermore that all circumstances of our current feeling, thinking, and acting will and must prove to be there in a still more lively and sharper way, only then are we saved, then the life in the here and now becomes the time of sowing for the joys or sorrows in the hereafter.

This expression had opened a new standpoint for looking at the matter, without spreading the proper conviction. They spoke back and forth so that it obtained the appearance as though they would never come to an understanding. The clergyman, who had almost exhausted his eloquence, said with firm voice, "Entirely forgotten is death; sharpened reminder for all we have done and omitted to do, is elevated life. On these two truths the laws of it and the necessity of virtue are founded." This remark was decisive. Everybody saw that without memory of the life in the here and now the hereafter was not to be considered to be a continuation of it. They were satisfied, and Bonhardt read the sixth paragraph[*].

The jurist, who found pleasure in the legalistic form of it, opened the discussion by saying, "Laws are present, that is not to be denied. To anyone who to some extent considers the course of nature with attentiveness, it becomes clear that through the entirety of creation an inescapable necessity reigns. Considering this, in so far as the human also stands under this necessity, a need arises which, like every striving of the powers of nature, must also be satisfied. It is only to be asked whether immortality can be brought under the rubric of such necessary laws and thereby described as a necessity."

---

[*]   See p. 61.

"It is a necessity," the merchant Glump replied with a raised voice. "Nobody can suppress the thirst for eternal life; and anyone who seeks to finally still it fades aways like the wanderer in the desert and dies in his living body in that he loses with the loss of the claim to eternity his human dignity and the lust for life."

"So it is," Bonhardt said. "The necessity of believing in immortality has been proved; our matter now is to get to know the laws under whose compliance the satisfaction is found. Reason and learnedness do not lead to the goal, as we see from the metaphor of the fountain. We must accordingly wait until a new path is revealed where we can see the truth without strange adornment and look into its pure mirror as part of God. But enough for today! What is yet dark will be made light by the following paragraphs." They parted and looked forward with pleasure to the following meeting.

Third Evening

Barely had the company gathered than the seventh paragraph* was read aloud. The newness of the path which the letter writer took up for the achieving of his goal strained the attention of all to a high degree. The jurist, after hearing it, immediately started to speak and said, "If I were to say that the content of this paragraph did not surprise me, I would have to be lying. Here the first knot which hinders us from free investigation is being sliced through. Previously we were bound to our fate by the belief in an all-too-great distance from God, or by his arbitrary influence; but now we obtain freedom not only in thinking and wanting, but also in believing in him. Certainly it may be beautiful to live in a realm of grace, if you belong directly amongst the most favoured for whom fortune falls in the lap without effort. Only just this realm, though many depend on it and think to honour God through the belief in it, goes against all concepts of justice. No father may make unequal portions. To each child he must, if he wants to be fair, give the full share in the inheritance. If then one would be, without merit, outfitted with strength and

---

*   See p. 61.

wisdom, while I languish in weakness and darkness, would I then not have the right to complain over being cut short? Anyone who struggles for proximity to God obtains it; but anyone who hopes with idle belief and humble behaviour for grace goes away empty. Herein lies the freedom to which the letter writer points when he says, 'True belief must not lose the freedom, it must insist on knowledge'."

Many did not want to see such a freedom. It fell especially hard on them to take from God all the administering of grace, since we see in the idea of an inexhaustible source of grace almost the most sublime characteristic of God. "How can you", the merchant Glump said, "praise the goodness and grace of a mighty one higher than if you said of him he was also kind and merciful towards the unworthy? And this most beautiful of all traits of infinite love should not be found in God?" The looks of all those present were directed at Bonhardt and expected from him enlightenment over the question that was placed before them.

He reflected for a few moments, and asked, "What would you say about a father who made every effort to educate his children well and at the same time to acquire as much wealth as to be able to look after them properly?"

Glump: "I would call him just."

Bonhardt: "Not also kind? Or gracious?"

Glump: "That too."

Bonhardt: "In what would lie the fairness and in what the grace?"

Glump: "The fulfilment of obligations is based on fairness; but if it happens out of love, on grace."

Bonhardt: "The wealth of the father, in the case he did not use it, belongs according to the strictest law to the children; thus here there can be no talk of grace."

Glump: "If fulfilment of obligations excludes grace, then you are right. Only the father can also do more than his duty, and in this case he is gracious."

Bonhardt: "Anyone can, if it is about the care of his own or even of others, say here duty ends. I suggest the instance of a father who possesses from birth already so much wealth that he did not need to acquire anything more; what would such a one have to do?"

Glump: "Care for his children, like the above."

Bonhardt: "Making equal or unequal parts?"

Glump: "Understandably equal ones."

Bonhardt: "But if one through a weakened health or lack of talent needed more than the others?"

Glump: "Then it would be a duty to make an exception."

Bonhardt: "I think here would be the opportunity to administer grace."

Glump: "Quite right."

Bonhardt: "But if the other children were against it?"

Glump: "Then the father would have to use his standing."

Bonhardt: "And fall out with his children? Perhaps starting lawsuits."

Glump: "I don't know how it would be helped in any other way."

Bonhardt: "Imagine a father who possesses such immeasurable riches that none of his children would ever be in a position to receive his share entirely, much less to use it."

Glump: "Then he would not need to give any more than to the others."

Bonhardt: "And the equal partition, what would it be, grace or fairness?"

Glump: "Fairness."

Bonhardt: "And could the father ever arrive at a case of having to be gracious?"

Glump: "In this case never."

Bonhardt: "And are you in a position to imagine God other than in the possession of such immeasurable riches of which the children are incapable of using the millionth part?"

Glump: "I cannot say no."

Bonhardt: "And what does the child of such a rich father have to do?"

Glump: "Make himself worthy of the father, seek his knowledge in order to become capable of taking possession of his share of the inheritance as much as possible."

Bonhardt: "Does grace or favour come into play anywhere here?"

Glump: "Up to now no. But to obtain the right knowledge would certainly be the highest grace though?"

Bonhardt: "Every child has amongst the treasures of his share of the inheritance a source of wisdom from which all knowledge flows."

Glump: "According to that we would have only to hold onto our share of the inheritance?"

Bonhardt: "So it is."

Glump: "But where does the love remain which binds God to humanity and humanity to God?"

Bonhardt: "God gave humanity everything he possesses out of love, the human was conceived and is thereby called upon to love."

Glump: "The matter sounds so natural and yet is so difficult to grasp! Why?"

Bonhardt: "We are used to being active with the senses, but not with the spirit. If we even once plan to work spiritually, then we need pen and paper in order to not forget the main clauses up to the end judgement and to always have them in view."

Glump: "How is that to be helped?"

Bonhardt: "Getting to know God in the share of the inheritance which he gifts us so that our feeling expresses: God is the eternal, kind giver and father."

Glump: "In what way is it possible to learn to recognise God himself through knowledge of our share of the inheritance?"

Bonhardt: "Through the idea that God gave himself to humanity through his spirit itself."

Glump: "I am satisfied and will seek to actively preserve these thoughts in myself."

Bonhardt: "Then you will achieve the freedom of life. Mystical binding to belief leads to narrow-mindedness and severity; rational belief to egotism and to the denial of God; free, living belief seeks satisfaction through knowledge of spiritual powers. It does not fear the light, but rather expects from it enlightenment and truth about the most important circumstances of existence and about the standpoint of the spiritual efficacy of humanity in relation to God."

Everybody seemed to be clear on the content of the seventh paragraph and prepared to hear the eighth*. It was read aloud and they marvelled at its brevity and soundness.

The clergyman was the first to break the silence, and said, "This paragraph sounds like an oracle, and it is difficult to say anything about it. Knowledge must come to us if we shall be placated over our destiny. Knowledge must be able to be granted to us if we are not to be cut short. Are these sentences so irrevocable that not even the slightest objection can be made? You should think it, and yet they are empty sentences if the test of them is not made through experience itself. But where to we find the test? And in what way can it be delivered?"

Since he did not seem to want to continue talking, Bonhardt continued. "You are right, the test must show us the correctness of the cited sentences. The letter writer specifies the path at the end of the paragraph when he says, 'True knowledge does without temporal knowledge, it penetrates into eternity and looks around there for what share the human has in it.' Here the necessity of a knowledge of eternal life answers us again, because we cannot obtain any contentment without certainty of it. Let us therefore pass on to the ninth paragraph† in which there are hints which are already raising a part of the curtain behind which the truth is concealed." He read it and continued straightaway to speak himself.

"Here we step into a world of miracles which, however, like the visible creation, moves according to pure laws of nature, and delivers their phenomena and products. Immortality, it says in the paragraph, is the goal of humanity, but also the greatest wonder of creation, but even the scholars believe in that. It is superfluous to remark how inconsequential it is to believe the most difficult thing, but consider the lesser difficulty to be impossible. Here it is mainly about how immortality is to be united with the course of nature and is to bring the miraculous under the laws of necessity."

---

*   See p. 62.
†   See p. 62.

The jurist responded here, "Immortality must be, and thus is not a miracle. Immortality must rest on unalterable laws of nature which exercise themselves like the chick leaps from the shell, otherwise it is impossible and based on hypotheses which break up and disappear like smoke in the wind."

The clergyman desired to speak and continued in the following manner, "In order to obtain a few results in the investigation of the object before us, we must arrive at an understanding over the concept of *miracle*. Miracle means in common life the direct effect of God on the course of nature, on the fates of entire peoples as well as individual humans, caused through the will of God, or through the desire and request of a people, a community, or a human. Since God exercises no arbitrariness, but rather has placed his will as irrevocable law in nature, his influence in respect to such miracles falls away by itself, and we have only to look around for the knowledge of those laws under which such miracle-like phenomena can result.

There are things in nature which are not to be measured with the usual yardstick. We must give a more correct meaning to the word miracle for our investigations and say: miracles are such phenomena whose origin and cause you do not know in general. To the common man the rotation of the earth about the sun and the turning on its axis is a miracle. To many the effects of electricity, of galvanism and magnetism are supernatural things. In this way of considering the miracle, we to not push away the supernaturalists completely, whereas we do not only not diminish the rights of reason, but rather open yet a new field of activity for it. Certainly it may not be easy to find the certain tracks on paths walked by so few; but to conclude we have reached the peak of all knowledge is too daring, too hubristic, all the more since even in our days the powers of natural history make an appearance, powers whose presence we would have denied in our youth for life and death. Who would have believed the steam from water exercised such a force and utility? Who would have even dreamed fifty years ago of seeing an entire city illuminated by gas? What discoveries have been made in the area of astronomy? No, we are not yet at the zenith of knowledge, and it is premature to deny powers which we are not yet in a position to comprehend in our limited state."

Bonhardt, in order to direct the discussion logically, now took the lead and said, "Since we are as one over the concept of *miracle*, it is to be asked whether immortality is surpassed somehow by a phenomenon of the miraculous, and whether we are justified in considering it to be the highest result of the power of creation familiar to us. If you lend me a few moments of your attention, I will try to give you the clearest possible information on this point.

The exit from the here and now to the hereafter evades the external experience in such a way that nobody can say such and such happens, in this or that way the human passes over into the eternal. Withdrawn from all visibility, this act must happen and cannot leave behind anything for us but the cold, rigid image of death. Every other phenomenon which we see in the area of the miraculous still bears in itself somewhere a sign of sensory, visible action, be it prayers, gestures, or touches whereby the result is produced. Considered from this point of view, we must declare immortality, the event withdrawn from all observation and imaginings, to be the highest miracle.

One has in more recent times pushed the miracles of Christ, in particular his healings through word, touch, and breathing on, into the realm of fables or folk tales invented by weak spirits, and not considered that he principally showed thereby his inner, high spiritual power. He showed before all of Judea that the human is capable of bringing into use the inflow and outflow of life not only on himself alone, but also on others and he is called to a freer activity than the usual life offers.

The human is built to breathe in everything which wafts about him. But not only the nose, no, all the senses and organs, the pores which go through the skin, even through the bones, are destined for this activity, and the breathing in uninterruptedly of finer air agreeing with their position and characteristics, and nourishing himself with it for a higher life. There, where the pores close and the breathing in and out is hindered, pains and illnesses occur. Now it is well-known that when the hand of a healthy person touches the sick part of the suffering person, the pain, at least for moments, stops. Let us assume one has practised the breathing in and out through the hand artificially, places it on the sick place of another; will the previously closed pores not open themselves through the penetration of this breath, begin their activity again, and in this way vanish the pains? Let us imagine to this end a human, even a God-man, who sound in soul and body, uncorrupted by the influences of the times which weaken human nature through opulence, falsehood, vain doctrines, and harmful pleasures, let us imagine such a one whose inner-being feels its power in all parts and understands how to share it with others by means of that living breath; then effects must follow which appear incomprehensible to everybody and appear to be caused directly by the creator."

The company had listened to this talk in astonishment. Even as Bonhardt fell silent, they could not give words to their astonishment. Finally the clergyman said, "There is a higher, a divine doctrine of nature to which you have shown us admission. I acknowledge, even if still wavering, the divine power of humans and regret only that one has so rarely and so late first made us familiar with it."

All shared the feelings of the clergyman, and the discussion concluded for the day full of joy and thankfulness for the explanations received over the most important characteristics of human nature.

Fourth Evening

Barely had the company gathered than the tenth paragraph* was recited. It was listened to without special interest, and hence Bonhardt saw himself obliged to explain its content more precisely.

He began, "We hear in life the word *holy* quite often without thinking about the true sense of it. We speak of the Holy God, God himself we call holy. For humans often regions, names, and even memories are holy. Now it is to be asked, does the predicate *holy* attach to individual feelings and ideas of every single person? To some something is holy,

---

* See p. 63.

to others not. God, the holiest of all, is by many considered to not be holy. The concept *holy* refers accordingly more to us ourselves than to an object. That which touches our dearest interests is holy to us without consideration of the judgement of others. When someone now asks, what is holy not only to the individual, but to all of humanity, then the frank answer is: the certainty of life, in one word, immortality.

The Bible is called the holy scripture. In order to deserve this name, it must contain the means of satisfying our holiest wishes. When this is the case, then it is wrong to treat it only as a commentary of moral principles, religious customs, and prescriptions, because it lies before us in any case as a book of law in which the conditions and principles of immortality are contained. From this it emerges that the Bible can be interpreted neither rationally, supernaturally, nor mythically, but only practically through the exercise of its laws of life.

In order to arrive here at a clearer view, we must emphasise the essential difference between art and science and seek the correct idea in their comparison.

The nature of science is theory and application at the same time in that it is fulfilled by the founding of its laws. Art stands in respect to practice above science because it uses this only as means to assist the flight of enthusiasm and at the same time to set appropriate limits. The artist must stand far above the school so that you do not perceive in him anymore either theory or rule. Science occupies understanding and reason, art symbolises both in order to also act spiritually on the feelings, the actual life source of humans. Now it is to be asked under which category the exercise of Biblical laws is to be brought? — The aim of religion is not to enrich understanding and reason, but rather to ennoble the disposition and to make it receptive for the influence of God and eternity. Hence the Bible can never be treated, discussed, and shown scientifically, but can well as a result of a higher, divine artistic power."

Many members expressed their doubts over these remarks. Accustomed to considering understanding and reason as the highest powers of human perfection, it seemed to them a degradation of the Bible to place it in the class of works of art. The clergyman expressed his opinion over it frankly, and said,

"Artworks are births of the time, serviceable to the moods of the viewer as of the artist, and hence the Bible, as an outflow of eternal wisdom, can never be set in a category with them."

Bonhardt responded, "Art is eternal, even if artworks and artists pass away. Wisdom is eternal; but since artwork, artist, and tool are just one thing here, the student of wisdom raises himself above the times, and passes over, binding himself with the matter itself, into immortality."

Several did not yet want to see the light of this claim. The clergyman said, "According to such a view art stands above science, and we are required to consider God himself as an artist."

"And is he not then?", Bonhardt replied. "Must we not admire him as architect of creation? Does he not stand before us in this characteristic as the most unattainable artist?

Not only did he think up and draft the plan or sketch of creation; no, he built it, produced it. For this reason the scientific treatment of the Bible relates to the fulfilled law like the sketch to the completed building."

They did not remember anything more, and declared the paragraph sufficiently discussed. Bonhardt read the eleventh[*] out.

The impression which this paragraph brought forth was insignificant. The jurist said, "That sounds like theorems, and yet no doctrine is contained in it. It is an attempt to bring history, morals, and law under one idea without the necessity of expressing this union." Another said, "To me this paragraph seems like a hieroglyph which has its solution in the recognition of the lines binding it." — The doctor of law replied, "I cannot agree with the above views. History, morals, and law are connected in the most natural way, and if you want to offer me a few moments of your attention, I hope to portray the matter clearly.

The paragraph says: The Bible as law is at the same time history. Had the letter writer expressed it as follows, the history in the Bible contains at the same time the law in itself, then the sentence would stand closer already to our sort of concept; for to spread commands or laws in historical form

---

[*]   See p. 63.

would often be much more expedient than the dry, incomprehensible determinations. Were to every law which you gave added at the same time a history agreeing with it, then it would be easy for all, even the uneducated, to understand and to follow the use of it. In this way, as stated above, law and history unite in the most natural of ways. Just as closely lies the tying of morals to them both. Meticulous exercise both of the laws of nature and social arrangements are morals in the simplest sense of the word; since now history makes us familiar with the laws as duties and with the morals as exercise of them, all three are so closely bound that no one thing may be lacking for our aims."

"As clearly as the speaker before me has expressed himself," one of the members responded, "it sounds though too juridicial. We are accustomed through the discussion of the earlier paragraphs to a certain swing, I would like to say a sort of poetic portrayal, so that such a calm explanation cannot suffice for us, and hence I ask in everyones' names for our friend Bonhardt to give us instruction over this."

Bonhardt accepted and began, "The above explanation is so clear that nothing more is to be added to its essence. I will allow myself to just touch on one point, namely that the law which we receive through history is neither to be recognised nor fulfilled without morals.

Social institutions also require social virtues which are only written in the heart, never in a book though. The exercise of such virtues is based on an inherent law of human love and morality which we describe with no other name than *morals*. The admittance to this internal book of law is the first step to the actual life. The more we get to know this internal voice of law, and the closer we bring it to social institutions, then the purer our moral state becomes, and the more suited we become to grasp the law of the eternal judge who has his voice in us and to unite ourselves with him through its fulfillment. In this respect this paragraph concludes itself and leads us over to the twelfth*, which thus begins: It is the law which lies between rationalism and supernaturalism and indicates to us the spirit of the Bible."

---

*   See p. 63.

He read it to the end and awaited the judgement of the members. It did not take long before one rose and said, "The end discussion of the previous paragraph also explains the start of the one we have just heard. If the eternal judge can speak in us, then his language is also the law which is announced through the entire Bible. No chapter is found where there are no hints of a voice which comes from eternity and expresses itself as law and lawgiver. On what laws of nature this rests, I cannot indeed fathom yet, but they must be present and be investigated, otherwise the Bible, this holy book, could not with such consequence trace back its numerous phenomena to the same basic cause."

The jurist began to speak and said, "This paragraph is the most important of all those over which we have spoken so far. It combines things which are not only horror to the usual researcher, but contradictions. It says within: Here we should get to know the interaction between matter and spirit, between form and God, between striving for freedom and its possession. What does matter have to do with spirit? Who can imagine God under a form? What gaps lie between striving for freedom and its possession? I am incapable of answering these questions and am convinced, if they are to be answered, there is only *one* in our company who is in a position to; hence I ask him in everyones' name to give us if not a solution then hints about this puzzle." Bonhardt saw all eyes directed at himself and made himself heard in the following way.

"I want to give some indications, to the extent my power and language allows it. The putting together of matter and spirit appears strange to you, and yet matter can only move and be brought into action and be animated through spirit. Who is capable of giving the hand a specific direction without the action of the spirit? Who can chisel a stone or draw a picture without it? It pushes through from the innermost life as far as the rawest tips of the touch. Here I do not yet want to mention the effect on foreign matter, on objects outside us; I must only say so much as that matter, without spiritual influence, would be a raw, stiff clump, without power of procreation, without vegetation and life.

It is the same story between form and God. Who created the world? God. Where did he take his model from? Within himself. Since he took the model from within himself, will there not be in every form which is to be perceived in his creation a sign of his being, of his word?

The interaction between striving for freedom and its possession hardly needs mentioning. Will the spirit of the eternal father, the eternal original power which gives to those who ask earnestly for their daily bread, not also gift spiritual freedom if the request is spoken in the spirit. The human can attain everything if he turns himself in the language of feeling to God and thereby connects himself with the spirit which is God in the being of the father from eternity to eternity."

Everybody was very pleased by this explanation, and decided, in order to not extinguish the impression, not to hear any further discussion. They showed Bonhardt their thanks, and parted in the happy expectation of being edified another time again in a similar way.

Fifth Evening

Hardly had the company assembled after four days than they were urging for the reading aloud of the thirteenth[*] paragraph. Bonhardt complied with their wishes and said, after he had finished, "What we have heard and discussed up to now, we must look on as preparation for penetrating into the spirit of the Bible. Now it appears as law and lays before us a canon according to which we can test the phenomena of human nature and at the same time identify to what degree we have remained true to the end goal of life or not. It is to be asked therefore mainly whether such a canon is founded in history, and with what means our ancestors were in a position to draft it and to obtain recognition for it.

With everything that the human undertakes, he has the end goal and the highest possible perfection before his eyes. Indeed the performance mostly remains far behind his ideal, the design of which he can give with fair certainty of what degree of perfection his work would possess if he could have ap-

---

[*] See p. 64.

plied more practice, more ability, a calmer disposition, more persistence and diligence to it. Such a, I would like to say, philosophically designed goal already delivers much material for the establishment of a canon; if we finally still have opportunity to see completed works, or to purify our views in living images, then it must be possible for us to imagine a highest state and to form a perfect ideal or a canon."

As clearly as this talk had analysed the matter, it did not yet seem to find the proper acknowledgement from the company. A few doubted the historical grounding of such a canon. Others even thought the entire matter rested only on an arbitrarily thought-up idea whose realisation belonged in the realm of fantasy. The jurist claimed in contrast to be able to prove that the Greek artists possessed a canon for the execution of their artworks. The clergyman, who was thrilled not only by the possibility, but also by the truth of what was stated, said, "How can we doubt a matter which has factually propagated as far as our own times? Even now you separate the Bible into apocryphal and canonical books. From where could this expression come, if it did not originate from an ancient, canonical law?"

This question, because it brought the disputed object as it were before the mind, tipped the scales. Everybody recalled how often they had heard in their lives already about canonical principles, canonical articles of belief, etc. and gave their agreement to the paragraph. It was decided to have the fourteenth* read aloud and to perhaps draw from this still clearer indications.

Bonhardt read. Deep silence reigned at the conclusion of it. Finally the clergyman broke the silence and said solemnly, "Here there is nothing to ask or to discuss. The three sorts of God's children are the pillars of the Bible without which even Christianity has no foundation and no solidity."

Since none of the members made any move to speak, Bonhardt continued, "There is a God; who will deny it? There is immortality; we all believe in it. But immortality is the most wonderful thing in creation, and hence we have no cause to doubt the possibility of any Biblical miracle. The creature of

---

* See p. 64.

humanity is not immortal; all of which it consists returns to the basic elements and no trace of the former individual is to be seen anymore. Immortality is attained when the spirit in the creature produces a new abiding body which is connected with the creature and takes up its feelings and thoughts into itself. The purer and more distant the etheric-spiritual body is from the creaturely, and the rawer the creaturely one is, then the more imperfect becomes the connection between both and the more uncertain the state of eternal life. But the more creaturely the etheric, new body and the purer the creaturely, then the more certain we are of the union and the more definitely we may count on taking our entire individuality across. Let us imagine the etheric body as a fine, light spirit which shall unite with impure, thick water, the creaturely body, and we will endeavour in vain. The light spirit floats above, the water remains below, and if we shake both to the bottom, then we will see that they separate entirely and in the water not even a trace of spirit remains, in the latter though not even the slightest part of water remains. But when we make the attempt and thicken the spirit with more substantial alcoholic fluids, but at the same time purify and distil the water, then both parts will merge in such a way as if they had been at origin only one. The first case describes the coldest indifferentism and complete dominance of the senses; the second, however, is the culmination point of human ennoblement where the creature vanquishes even death and does not see decomposition.

There is a rebirth in the spirit. The procreation of an etheric body through the spirit is this rebirth. This etheric body arises like the creaturely in the womb, and grows from there through all the parts and organs of life. Since the procreation of an as it were divine body is grounded in nature, and the nearing of it to the creature serves to ennoble us, we are not drawing conclusions against reason when we say that with appropriate conditions the etheric body, touched by corporeal nourishment, consolidates itself so much that it, a human creature produced by the spirit, is capable of leaving its maternal residence and stepping out into the external world equipped with human characteristics. If the one is so, the other can and must even be under favourable circumstances too.

This is, even if an imperfect one, yet an indication agreeing with nature of the manner of arising of the second class of the children of God. The first must be possible, otherwise no humans would be present. The beginnings of almost all peoples, all mythologies and mysteries teach it and portray it under vivid symbols and parables. And in this respect we must, where all peoples and times agree, not be scared of being deceived, and must consider that without the teaching of nature such an agreement could never have taken place."

Everyone thanked him for this talk which led them onto the trail of a matter which they had also previously not had the slightest idea of. One said, "From this moment on I swear on the entire contents of the Bible." — Another said, "Only now do I begin to be a Christian, because I know on what foundations Christianity rests. — The clergyman said, "I think we all would have first received baptism in this hour." "We have become humans," a fourth said, "and in this dignity we want to preserve ourselves and seek to perfect ourselves in order to see ourselves there again one day." "Amen," said the jurist, fetched a Bible from the table, placed his hand on it and called out loudly, "From today on I know you and vow to fulfill you as much as possible." "We vow the same," the others concurred, and thus the evening concluded in the sublime feeling of having found the signpost to life.

Sixth Evening

When the company had assembled again on the specified day, they discussed, in the view that the limit of the Bible were now described, the spirit of the last two paragraphs heard. Bonhardt brought to their attention that three paragraphs were not yet discussed and he considered it expedient to also bring the matter to an end the way they had begun. Many who no longer recalled the fifteenth paragraph* anymore were of the opinion that after what had been heard nothing more that was essential could follow. But Bonhardt

---

*   See p. 64.

declared that in order to close the Bible the three following paragraphs were necessary. They believed this assurance and he recited the fifteenth, which mentioned the kingdom of the angels and saints. With the first reading of the letter the company seemed not to have grasped the sense of this paragraph at all, so new and wondrous it now seemed to them.

Bonhardt saw this mood and said, "Here there is actually nothing to add and nothing to take away. It is a whole, but hanging together so gigantically that it dizzies the weak understandings of humans to imagine it. Life is everywhere, from the lowest to the highest, and nobody can say it is not possible, because we must also assume what we see realised in one endpoint of creation at the other endpoint. Strictly separated, floating around any heavenly body are circles on circles, strongholds on strongholds, they attach onto and intervene in the circles of other worlds, suns, and stars and, forming an immeasurable chain, share with one another their life potencies and powers so that every star, even our simple earth, absorbs into itself the influence of Sirius, of Orion, indeed of yet undiscovered universes. In the visible creation we see living beings for which the power of thought sees no possibility and no yardstick anymore. In the upper circles are beings of a spiritual sort which only our inner eye recognises. Over the possibility or impossibility, over the truth or falsity of them, nothing is to be said. It is, like everything in creation, and must be so because God can still be infinite and eternal, and in him there is no standstill and no emptiness. His life is poured out over all regions of creation and lifeless, unused space contradicts just as much his being as if we wanted to claim the sea was uninhabited because the blind do not see it and in the midst of the water no breathing of air is possible. But anyone who believes the words of the Bible needs no further proof, for it speaks of God on high, of an ascent to heaven, of a ninth heaven, of a new city of God which descends from heaven, of angels and saints above the worlds, in short, of a kingdom of light in which the purer angels and saints stand closer to the throne of the highest one than the less pure, but where everywhere the delights of worship and love are felt which the residents of light are capable of by virtue of their uplift. I conclude the discussion of this paragraph as the highest thing which the spiritual power of humanity is given for contemplation and for testing their sublime position, and pass over to the sixteenth[*]."

After he had read it out, he continued. "There is a kingdom of darkness which we can all be witness too if we look at ourselves only to some extent. Hate, revenge, and addiction to persecution do not come from God, but rather from the spirit of darkness. Where this kingdom lies is given variously. A few set it in the midpoint of matter, but others and Christ see it in the polar regions of the heavenly bodies where the circles of light do not fall into line with each other, forming by contrast pointed and even crooked angles in which life moves irregularly, where eternal coldness reigns and howling and chattering of teeth will be. I also conclude this paragraph because its truth, like the preceding, is more to be felt than expressed, and will speak full of conviction about the seventeenth[†], instead of any discussion, in the letter writer's own words:

These few lines are the outline of the Bible. Anyone who crosses out just one line has destroyed the Bible. They are the pillars of the Old and New Testaments, of which none may be removed without collapsing the whole into rubble. They are the law of which Christ himself said, anyone who dissolves the least of it is condemned to the eternal fire. What would the holy scripture be without Adam, the first born; the son of God blinded by Satan? Without him, the father of a numerous progeny dedicated to God? What would it be without Moses and the prophets? What without the spiritual power of Christ, with which he healed illnesses and commanded storms? Without his wisdom, with which he connected with the father and saw unveiled everything which was and will be? It would be the most incomplete book which we would have inherited from antiquity; a chaos of teachings and stories from which

---

[*]   See p. 65.
[†]   See p. 66.

96

nobody could draw salvation nor light. Any impartial person will see the inadmissibility of even only the slightest reform of the Bible and be forced either to completely deny it or to acknowledge it in its entirety."

Everybody shared his avowal, but suggested yet one more paragraph must follow which contains the single infallible proof of immortality. Bonhardt replied to this, "The proof is not expressed in that paragraph, but rather left over from it." He did not yet know whether and what he would say about it, and asked to close the discussion for today. The company parted with the request to be permitted to visit him again in four days.

***

3. Keystone of the Biblical Church

On the evening of the fourth day everybody had assembled and urged Bonhardt to read aloud the last paragraph[*]. He assented and said, "Everything which we have obtained through our investigations, as sublime as the results also were, can not serve you as irrevocable proof of immortality because according to the philosophical maxim everything which has come into being can die again. Even the spiritual (etheric) body is subject to the just expressed judgement, and can, just as it came into being, also dissolve again. There must accordingly have developed yet another power in the human by virtue of his rebirth which releases him from that maxim and bears in itself the guarantee of abidingness.

The power of which I speak works and weaves partly in the highest, partly in lesser perfection in the Bible and comprises at the same time the keystone to its symbolic law. The normal human sees the present through the sensory experience; the past through history; the reborn human sees into the future, and has thereby a guarantee for his future life.

The prophetic power knows fate and the incidents of days, weeks, months, and years in advance. If you say in ten years it will be so, then you may, when it occurs, also believe what it tells us in advance about thousands, about millions and myriads of years ahead, indeed even about eternity. This is the basis of the doctrine of immortality, without practical know-

---

[*] See p. 66.

ledge of which you would never, with all the yet so wondrous phenomena, have trusted yourself to teach immortality and lay claim to it."

"On what laws does the prophetic power of humanity rest?", the clergyman asked, and after him the entire company. Bonhardt replied, "It is what it is, and nobody can give a different explanation. It is a component part of human life, like seeing, hearing, and feeling. Can one give an explanation of them? Certainly not. They exist, we possess them and use their peculiarities according to irrevocable laws reigning in them themselves. So too the capability of gazing into the future, or of perceiving the course of its events. But because this sublime characteristic can be neither perceived through the senses, nor recognised through the powers of understanding, it was often denied for centuries and exercised under the rubric of a punishable mysticism which is only believed still by confused heads and exoteric enthusiasts. But suddenly, often after a long darkness, a genius would emerge again who bore witness to this highest good of human nature, had an effect, even if only on a few, through the example of a pure human nature, and illuminated for them the path forward in life."

Everybody thanked him for these words; but the jurist said, "That is not enough for us. You have accustomed us to seeing the truth of your explanations almost before our eyes, hence allow me to ask you to give us factual proofs over this point, and in bare words to ask whether you have seen into the future?"

Those present looked at this question with fixed and uncertain gaze at Bonhardt. But he directed his countenance upwards as if he were pondering the answer, and said with solemn seriousness, "Yes, the future unseals itself for me as often as I turn towards it."

An awed astonishment grasped the members after this confession. They set an unconditional trust on Bonhardt and believed his statement.

The clergyman raised his voice and said, "Our friend has unveiled to us everything which our souls needed; with this confession, however, he has vanquished everything which could still have given room for doubt."

The others affirmed this explanation gratefully and closed the evening in joyous recollection of what they had heard.

Seventh Evening

When the company had gathered again on the appointed day, the conversation turned to begin with, because they no longer saw any specific goal before themselves, to general topics. By and by, however, they came to speak again about the content of the letter and of the Bible. For this reason they also recalled the story of Jesus by Dr Strauss which had brought about the paragraphs and their discussion. For this reason they felt moved to likewise discuss and give judgement on the conclusion of that critical examination where the writer came closer to our views. The clergyman led the way in this respect and read aloud a few of the principal points of the book.

§ 150[*].

The incarnation of God is an incarnation of eternity.

If it is said of God that he is a spirit, the human is also spirit.[†]

God does not remain as a fixed and immutable Infinite encompassing the Finite, but enters into it.

If God then finds a passage from heaven to the grave, so must a way be discoverable for man from the grave to heaven: the death of the prince of life is the life of mortals.

§ 151.

Though I may see the human mind in its unity with the divine, in the course of the world's history, more and more completely establish itself as the power which subdues nature; this is quite another thing, than to con-

---

[*]   [Tr.: the numbering has been adjusted to reflect the fourth edition of the English translation of Strauss's work by George Eliot. The following excerpted passages are also taken from that edition except where they vary considerably from the first edition. Note that each paragraph is an excerpt from a longer passage in Strauss's original.]

[†]   [Tr.: my translation of the first edition. The fourth edition has: "When it is said of God that he is a Spirit, and of man that he also is a Spirit, it follows that the two are not essentially distinct."]

ceive a single man endowed with such power, for individual, voluntary acts.

This is the key to the whole of Christology, that, as
subject of the predicate which the church assigns to
Christ, we place, instead of an individual, an idea; but
an idea which has an existence in reality, not in the
mind only, like that of Kant. In an individual, a God-
man, the properties and functions which the church
ascribes to Christ contradict themselves; in the idea of
the race, they perfectly agree.

The science of our time cannot suppress the aware-
ness for any longer that the connection to the individual
belongs only to the temporal and racial form.[*]

Our age demands to be led in Christology to the idea
in the fact, to the race in the individual: a theology
which, in its doctrines on the Christ, stops short at him
as an individual, is not properly a theology, but a
homily.

The clergyman continued, "Such sentences show how serious it must have been for the author, with every renunciation
of the miraculous and of the unique, to rescue the sacred from
the Biblical truths and to just portray it under another form.
Now I ask, is reality in his deductions? And what profit arises
to Christianity if you withdraw all individual product from the
gospels and transfer it to an idea?"

Bonhardt felt compelled to answer these questions, and responded, "If we return to our earlier discussion in which immortality was expressed as the wish and goal of humanity,
then we will be in a position to easily judge the cited passages.

'The incarnation of God is an incarnation of eternity.' —
Who will deny that? Through the spirit and the word the human was incarnated, thus God is in the human from the start.
Likewise: 'If it is said of God that he is a spirit, the human is
also spirit.' — Only the spirit can think spirit, and hence this
verdict is as true as if I said the circle is a round figure. Just as

---

[*]   [Tr.: my translation of the first edition. The fourth edition has: "This alone is the
absolute sense of Christology: that it is annexed to the person and history of one
individual, is a necessary result of the historical form which Christology has
taken."]

true is the sentence that 'God does not remain as a fixed and immutable Infinite encompassing the Finite, but enters into it.' But to say if 'God then finds a passage from heaven to the grave, so must a way be discoverable for man from the grave to heaven' is too daring because from the perfect surely something great can arise, but not from the imperfect. But be that as it may, for our persistence after the temporal death such sentences give no guarantee. They are logically correct, but not practically proven. With each it is to be said: it can be true, but also not be true. No trace of the life power is present in it, the power on which, when our power of thought is no longer capable of expressing or interpreting it anymore, we could support ourselves and transfer our feelings, our ego, in one word, our individuality to it.

What is life? By what do we recognise that we are living? Through the feeling which expresses itself in the external senses and through the ability to distinguish, compare, and think about sensory ideas. Can this activity keep itself alive in the grave? We have already seen above how impossible that is. Different, inner senses must arise which takes over all the functions of the external ones so that we become capable of being active with those, the inner ones, and of putting our ego there at will; then we can, when the moment of parting arrives, go over into those senses, into the powers of life of the etheric body and fly ourselves with them into eternity. Of all these necessary requirements not the slightest is to be found in the cited Christology, and hence it contradicts the spirit of the Bible which wants nothing else but to lead us on the canonical path to immortality.

Over the sentences from § 151 much has already been spoken and weighed in other writings and company. But as magnificent as the idea may also be of expecting from the whole, from the mass, what can only be portrayed by individuals, we never find it realised in experience. When we see ourselves in the areas of art where idealising appears to be required exercise, we will find the confirmation that everything strives for idealised detail and the artist is only then convinced of having achieved the goal of his art when he has portrayed the characteristics of a genre in an individual work of art. Not in the mass, but in the individual does the excellence of any class, any art or science show itself. Homer is still the ideal of the poet. Newton, Kepler, and others stand as isolated heroes above the mass. Shakespeare gleams as writer of tragedies so brightly that you consider him still to be impossible to reach, much less to surpass. Does not in Mozart's genius lie the power of harmony and melody in its entire fullness and serve the others as a model for their work? Should that which shows itself everywhere as truth not apply as law in the area of human ennoblement? No, in the individual the noble of the race must present itself. The mass floats on the surface and only gazes up in order to investigate whether not one of its race rises from the dust; when they find none, then they reassure themselves and consider rising higher to be impossible; but once one appears who senses the courage, strength, and zeal in themselves to examine the human nature in himself, then he gazes on the masses only in order to collect from the millions of individuals the traits to unite in one image which can serve for him as canon, as law, to examine in himself what the human is capable of and how high he stands in the ranks of the saints of God.

It is an old doctrine: whoever strives for human knowledge should learn to recognise themselves. Many want to dispute this basic principle in that they claim only in all things is all contained. To them I give the story of a wise man and his student to consider, who on their wanderings came near to a small forest whose type of wood they did not know, but the teacher said to the student, 'Give me that information two days from now.'

The student went and ordered woodcutters in order to have the trees of the little forest cut down for the purpose of his investigation. The hired men were already intending to start their destructive business when the wise man stepped amongst them and called out, 'Stop!'. 'What sacrilege are you starting on?', he continued, turning towards the student.

The latter answered, 'At your command I want to examine the wood in this little forest.'

Wise man: 'And for that you need such destruction?'

Student: 'Of course, because I cannot fulfill your command otherwise.'

Wise man: 'There is only one type of wood in the little forest. Investigate one tree, then you will know them all.'

The student gave a doubtful look, but saw after some consideration that the master was right and asked, 'Which tree should I have cut down?' The teacher replied, 'The healthiest and the most perfectly grown.' The former followed this doctrine and brought the desired explanation the next day.

In every individual everything is united which the race has in it. In order to get to know humanity in its perfection, we are directed to ourselves because no other way lets us see into the lines of its heart. Anyone who realises in himself all the characteristics of his nature is in a position to account for the worth of humanity and to determine the relationship in which he stands to God. Such a one lights the way as an ordained one for the masses, he teaches them as his congregation to break through the dividing wall which separates us from eternity, and realises in this way the concept of every religion in that he establishes the Christian one in its undiminished and divine rights."

The jurist desired to speak and began, "This sequence of truths is so clear and correct that nothing can be said against it. But I would wish to be able to raise a doubt in order to make the Bible secure from any attack. It is reproached, and indeed not without good reason, for genealogical and chronological inaccuracies. How did these arise? And how are they to be connected with the divine truths contained in it?"

Bonhardt responded, "You should not have to answer to such reproaches at all because here an agreement was absolutely not possible. The books of the law were closed to the followers of Christ and they could therefore not draw genealogy and chronology from writings, but rather only from their memory and oral statements. Furthermore they did not have the opportunity to compare their gospels because each was written in a different place, at a different time, and in different communities. Their main goal was to describe the consummate historical image of the fulfilled canonical law, and to put it down for their brothers in faith for teaching and imitation. Such they did achieve, for everywhere they sacrificed to the crucified saviour and endeavoured to take up his sublime characteristics into themselves. They wrote for pure hearts and not for an age of speculation and criticism. They did what they could, and when they came to points where the spirit filled them, they wrote with a clarity and fullness so that Biblical diction still belongs in the sphere of the classics.

What else shall I say? It is an eternal word that is God which teaches the human and shows him the path of life.

There is a wisdom which flows from the word that is God, but remains closed to cleverness and science.

It, the law which stems from wisdom, is only given to the etheric, new-born body to fathom; hence nobody dares to explain the law before they have attained this state.

It, wisdom, shall teach and guide us. It shall come to us in its pure brilliance so that we gaze into it and reach in its spirit those climes where there is no death and no transformation anymore."

In such a way the discussion of the letter concluded, and the company was so moved that they considered each other in future not only to be friends, but to be brothers and fellow comrades of a divine life in which they, standing above transience, recognised eternity as their goal and their home.

***

**Other works by Johann Baptist Krebs
(originally published in German under
the pseudonym of J. B. Kerning)
published by K A Nitz**

Paths to Immortality
Based on the Undeniable Powers
of Human Nature

Christianity
or
God and Nature Only One
Through the Word

The Missionaries
The Path to the Teaching Profession
of Christianity